300 FANTASTIC FACTS

BUGS

300 FANTASTIC FACTS

BUGS

Written by: Camilla de la Bedoyere, Steve Parker

Miles Kelly

First published in 2016 by Miles Kelly Publishing Ltd
Harding's Barn, Bardfield End Green, Thaxted, Essex, CM6 3PX, UK

Copyright © Miles Kelly Publishing Ltd 2016

2 4 6 8 10 9 7 5 3 1

Publishing Director Belinda Gallagher
Creative Director Jo Cowan
Editorial Director Rosie Neave
Designer Andrea Slane
Cover Designer Rob Hale
Image Manager Liberty Newton
Production Elizabeth Collins, Caroline Kelly
Reprographics Stephan Davis, Jennifer Barker, Thom Allaway
Consultants Camilla de la Bedoyere, Steve Parker, Barbara Taylor

All rights reserved. No part of this publication may be reproduced, stored in a retrieval system, or transmitted by any means, electronic, mechanical, photocopying, recording or otherwise, without the prior permission of the copyright holder.

ISBN 978-1-78209-762-4

Printed in China

British Library Cataloguing-in-Publication Data
A catalogue record for this book is available from the British Library

Made with paper from a sustainable forest

www.mileskelly.net

Contents

BUGS
- Insects everywhere — 6
- How insects grow — 8
- Getting about — 10
- Champion leapers — 12
- Super sprinters — 14
- Watery wonders — 16
- Brilliant burrowers — 18
- Bloodthirsty bugs — 20
- Veggie bugs — 22
- Stings and things — 24
- Clever colonies — 26
- Where am I? — 28
- Great pretenders — 30
- Stay or go? — 32
- Noisy neighbours — 34
- Meet the family! — 36
- Friends and foes — 38

SPIDERS
- What is a spider? — 40
- Shapes and sizes — 42
- Fearsome family — 44
- Super spider senses — 46
- Smooth movers — 48
- Spider mates — 50
- Spiderlings — 52
- Where spiders live — 54
- Super silk — 56
- Weaving and building — 58
- On the menu — 60
- On the run — 62
- Death by stealth — 64
- Orb-web spiders — 66
- Funnel web spiders — 68
- Widows and wolves — 70
- Jumping spiders — 72
- Tarantulas — 74
- Spiders and us — 76
- SOS – save our spiders — 78

BUTTERFLIES & MOTHS
- Scale wings — 80
- Moth or butterfly? — 82
- A closer look — 84
- Super senses — 86
- Food and feeding — 88
- Getting together — 90
- Growing up — 92
- Clever caterpillars — 94
- Families of moths — 96
- Butterfly families — 98
- Cunning camouflage — 100
- Survival tricks — 102
- On the wing — 104
- The greatest traveller — 106
- We are the champions — 108
- Evolution long ago — 110
- Habitats galore — 112
- From mountains to cities — 114
- Dangers past and present — 116
- Hopes for the future — 118

INDEX — 120
ACKNOWLEDGEMENTS — 122

BUGS

1 **Insects are among the most numerous and widespread animals on Earth.** They form the largest of all animal groups, with millions of different kinds, or species, which live almost everywhere in the world. But not all creepy-crawlies are insects. Spiders belong to a different group called arachnids, and millipedes are in yet another group.

▶ Cockchafers are insects, as shown by their wings and six legs. Also called chafers, cockchafers belong to the largest subgroup of insects, the beetles.

Insects everywhere

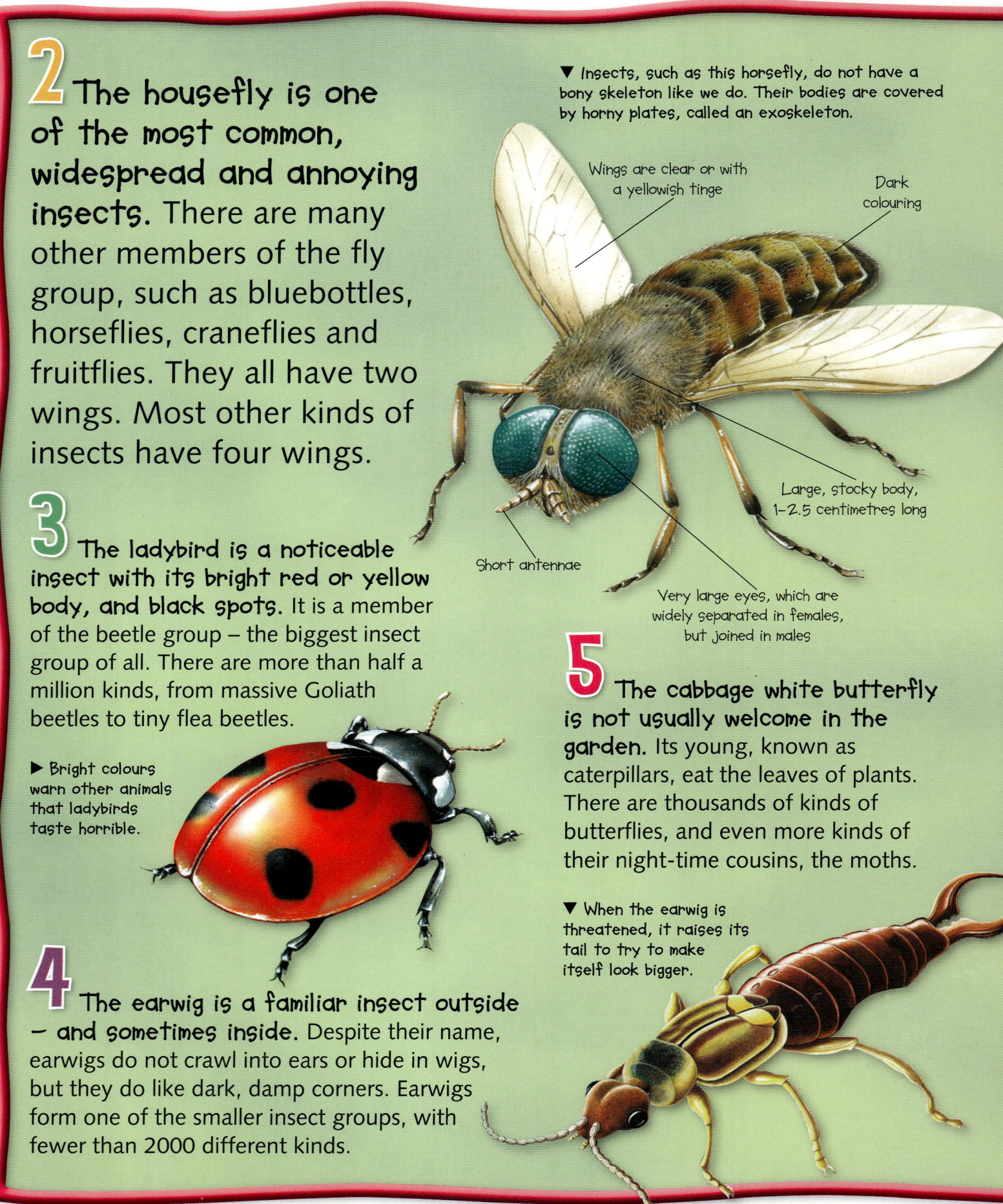

2 **The housefly is one of the most common, widespread and annoying insects.** There are many other members of the fly group, such as bluebottles, horseflies, craneflies and fruitflies. They all have two wings. Most other kinds of insects have four wings.

▼ Insects, such as this horsefly, do not have a bony skeleton like we do. Their bodies are covered by horny plates, called an exoskeleton.

Wings are clear or with a yellowish tinge

Dark colouring

Short antennae

Very large eyes, which are widely separated in females, but joined in males

Large, stocky body, 1–2.5 centimetres long

3 **The ladybird is a noticeable insect with its bright red or yellow body, and black spots.** It is a member of the beetle group – the biggest insect group of all. There are more than half a million kinds, from massive Goliath beetles to tiny flea beetles.

► Bright colours warn other animals that ladybirds taste horrible.

4 **The earwig is a familiar insect outside – and sometimes inside.** Despite their name, earwigs do not crawl into ears or hide in wigs, but they do like dark, damp corners. Earwigs form one of the smaller insect groups, with fewer than 2000 different kinds.

5 **The cabbage white butterfly is not usually welcome in the garden.** Its young, known as caterpillars, eat the leaves of plants. There are thousands of kinds of butterflies, and even more kinds of their night-time cousins, the moths.

▼ When the earwig is threatened, it raises its tail to try to make itself look bigger.

BUGS

6 **Ants are fine in the garden or wood, but are pests in the house.** Ants, bees and wasps make up a large insect group with some 130,000 different kinds. Most can sting, although many are too small to hurt people. However, some types, such as bulldog ants, have a painful bite.

▶ Ants use their antennae and sense of touch as a means of communication. These ants are forming a 'living bridge' so their fellow workers can cross a gap to reach food.

7 **The scorpionfly has a nasty-looking sting on a long curved tail.** It flies or crawls around bushes and weeds during summer. Only the male scorpionfly has the red tail. It looks like the sting of a scorpion, but is harmless.

SPOT THE INSECTS!
Have you seen any insects so far today? Maybe a fly whizzing around the house or a butterfly flitting among the flowers? On a warm summer's day you will probably spot lots of different insects. On a cold winter's day there are fewer insects about – most are hiding away or have not hatched out of their eggs.

9

How insects grow

▼ The scarlet lily beetle lays her eggs directly onto the lily leaves, which the grubs will eat when they hatch.

8 Nearly all insects begin life inside an egg. The female insect usually lays her eggs in an out-of-the-way place, such as under a stone, leaf or bark, or in the soil.

9 Courtship is a dangerous time for the male praying mantis. The female is much bigger than the male and, as soon as they have mated, she may eat him!

10 Usually a female insect mates with a male insect before she can lay her eggs. The female and male come together to check they are both the same kind of insect and are healthy. This is known as courtship. Butterflies often flit through the air together in a 'courtship dance'.

11 When some types of insects hatch, they do not look like their parents. A young beetle, butterfly or fly is soft-bodied, wriggly and worm-like. This young stage is called a larva. A beetle larva is called a grub, a butterfly larva is a caterpillar and a fly larva is a maggot.

◀ Large caterpillars always eat into the centre of the leaf from the edge. Caterpillars grasp the leaf with their legs, while their specially developed front jaws chew their food.

BUGS

1. The butterfly swallows air, expands its body and splits its chrysalis open
2. It struggles free of the casing
3. The butterfly clings to the chrysalis
4. Blood is pumped into the wings, which stretch and stiffen
5. In half an hour, the wings are full size. Once dry, the butterfly is able to fly

▲ This viceroy butterfly is emerging from its chrysalis.

12 The larva eats and eats. It sheds its skin several times so it can grow. Then it changes into the next stage of its life, called a pupa. The pupa has a hard outer case that stays still and inactive. Inside, the larva is changing shape again – this is known as metamorphosis.

13 At last the pupa's case splits open and the adult insect crawls out. Its body, legs and wings spread out and harden. Now the insect is ready to find food and a mate.

14 Some kinds of insects change shape less as they grow. When a cricket or grasshopper hatches, it looks similar to its parents, but it may not have wings.

15 The young cricket eats and eats, and sheds (or moults) its skin several times as it grows. Each time it looks more like its parent. A young insect that resembles an adult is called a nymph. At the last moult it becomes a fully formed adult, ready to feed and breed.

◄ Most crickets, as well as grasshoppers and locusts, moult between five and eight times before adulthood.

Getting about

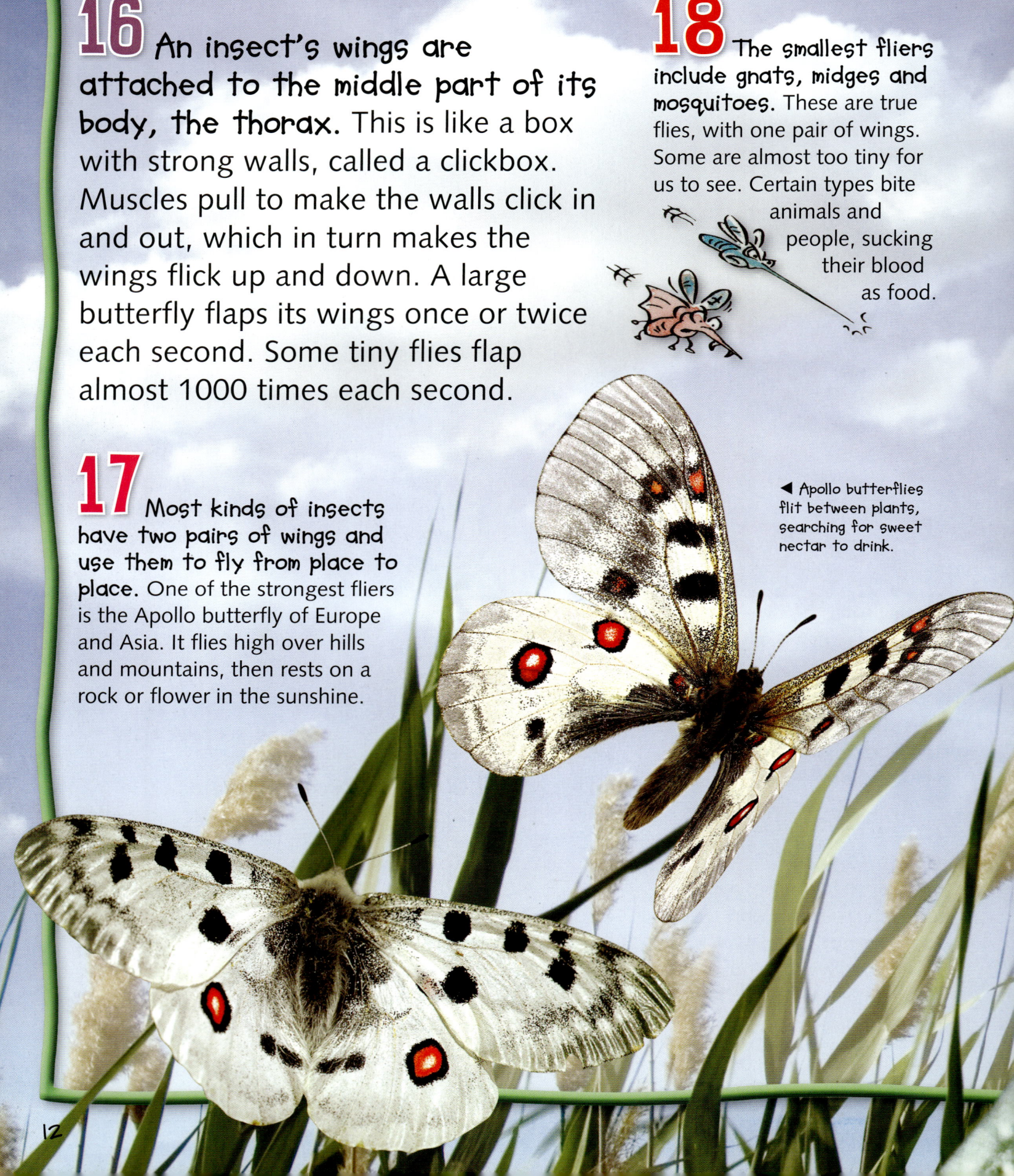

16 **An insect's wings are attached to the middle part of its body, the thorax.** This is like a box with strong walls, called a clickbox. Muscles pull to make the walls click in and out, which in turn makes the wings flick up and down. A large butterfly flaps its wings once or twice each second. Some tiny flies flap almost 1000 times each second.

17 **Most kinds of insects have two pairs of wings and use them to fly from place to place.** One of the strongest fliers is the Apollo butterfly of Europe and Asia. It flies high over hills and mountains, then rests on a rock or flower in the sunshine.

18 **The smallest fliers include gnats, midges and mosquitoes.** These are true flies, with one pair of wings. Some are almost too tiny for us to see. Certain types bite animals and people, sucking their blood as food.

◀ Apollo butterflies flit between plants, searching for sweet nectar to drink.

BUGS

19 **A few insects lack wings.** They are mostly very small and live in the soil, such as bristletails and certain aphids. One kind of bristletail is the silverfish – a small, shiny, fast-running insect.

◀ Dragonflies catch prey in a 'basket' formed by their legs.

▶ Silverfish are nocturnal, which means they are mainly active at night.

20 **A fast and fierce flying hunter is the dragonfly.** Its huge eyes spot tiny prey such as midges and mayflies. The dragonfly dashes through the air, turns at speed, grabs the victim and flies back to a perch to eat its meal.

21 **Some insects flash bright lights as they fly.** The firefly is not a fly, but a type of beetle. Male fireflies 'dance' in the air at dusk, the rear parts of their bodies glowing on and off about once each second. Female fireflies stay on twigs and leaves, and glow in reply as part of their courtship.

▼ Each kind of firefly has its own pattern of flashes.

QUIZ

1. How many wings do most insects have?
2. Where on its body are an insect's wings attached?
3. Which part of the firefly glows in the dark?

Answers:
1. Two pairs
2. Its middle, called the thorax
3. Rear parts

Champion leapers

22 Many insects move around mainly by hopping and jumping, rather than flying. They have long, strong legs and can leap great distances, especially to avoid enemies and escape from danger. Grasshoppers are up to 15 centimetres long and some types can jump more than 3 metres. The grasshopper often opens its brightly patterned wings briefly as it leaps, giving a flash of colour.

23 The springtail jumps with its tail, rather than its legs. The rear part of its body is shaped like a V or Y. It is folded under the body until it flicks down and flips the insect through the air. Springtails are as long as this letter 'l' but some can leap more than 5 centimetres!

Long, hind legs for leaping

Lower leg section, or tibia

Foot, or tarsus

Two sets of short front legs for landing and walking

◀ The grasshopper straightens each section of its back legs in turn, from the large upper section, to the lower one, while the foot holds firm until take-off.

BUGS

▲ Froghoppers take just one five-hundredth of a second to get airborne.

24 **The greatest insect jumpers for their size are fleas, and also the froghopper.** This small sap-sucking bug can leap over 70 centimetres high – more than 100 times its own body length.

Large eyes to focus on where to land

Wings folded against body

Upper leg section, or femur

QUIZ

1. Does the springtail jump using its head or tail?
2. How high is a froghopper able to leap?
3. What does a click beetle do when it's in danger?

Answers:
1. Uses its tail 2. 100 times its own body length 3. It plays dead

① Click beetle plays dead
② Arches its body and flicks up
③ Lands right way up on leaf

25 **The click beetle, or skipjack, is another insect leaper.** This beetle is about 12 millimetres long. When it is in danger it falls on its back and pretends to be dead. When the danger has passed, it slowly arches its body and straightens with a 'click'. It can flick itself about 25 centimetres into the air!

◀ The 'click' is from a joint between the first and second thorax parts.

Super sprinters

▶ Cockroaches are expert scavengers, able to live on tiny scraps of our food. Some kinds spread germs in their droppings.

26 Some insects rarely fly or leap. They prefer to run and run… all day, and sometimes all night too. Among the champion insect runners are cockroaches. There are about 4500 different kinds and they are tough and adaptable. Some live in soil or caves, but most scurry speedily across the ground and dart into narrow crevices, under logs, stones, cupboards – even beds!

BUGS

27 **One of the busiest insect walkers is the devil's coach-horse, which resembles an earwig.** It belongs to the group known as rove beetles, which walk huge distances to find food.

▼ The devil's coach-horse has powerful mouthparts to tear apart small caterpillars, grubs and worms.

28 **Some insects can run along smooth slippery surfaces, such as walls, windows or wet rocks.** Others can run along the beds of ponds and rivers. The stonefly nymph has big, strong, wide-splayed legs that grip even smooth stones in rushing streams.

◀ The stonefly nymph, the larva of the stonefly, scuttles over wet rocks and riverbeds searching for food.

29 **The green tiger beetle is an active hunter.** It races over open ground, chasing smaller creatures such as ants, woodlice, worms and little spiders. It has huge jaws for its size and rips apart any victim.

30 **Green tiger beetles are only 12–15 millimetres long.** However, they can run at about 60–70 centimetres per second – that's like a human sprinter running 100 metres in one second!

Watery wonders

▶ Pondskaters row on water with their rear four legs.

31 **Many kinds of insects live underwater in ponds, streams, rivers and lakes.** Some walk along the bottom, others swim strongly using their legs as oars to row through the water. The great diving beetle hunts small water creatures, such as tadpoles and baby fish. It can give a person a painful bite in self-defence.

32 **Some insects even walk on water.** The pondskater has a slim, light body with long, wide-splayed legs. It glides across the water surface 'skin' or film, known as surface tension. The pondskater is a member of the bug group of insects and eats tiny animals, which fall into the pond.

▶ The great diving beetle breathes air, which it collects and stores under the hard wing-cases on its back.

Large pincer-like mouthparts

INVESTIGATE

With help from a grown-up, fill a bowl of water and let the water settle. Investigate what you can place on top of the water that doesn't break the water tension. Try laying paper, plastic or grass on the water. What happens?

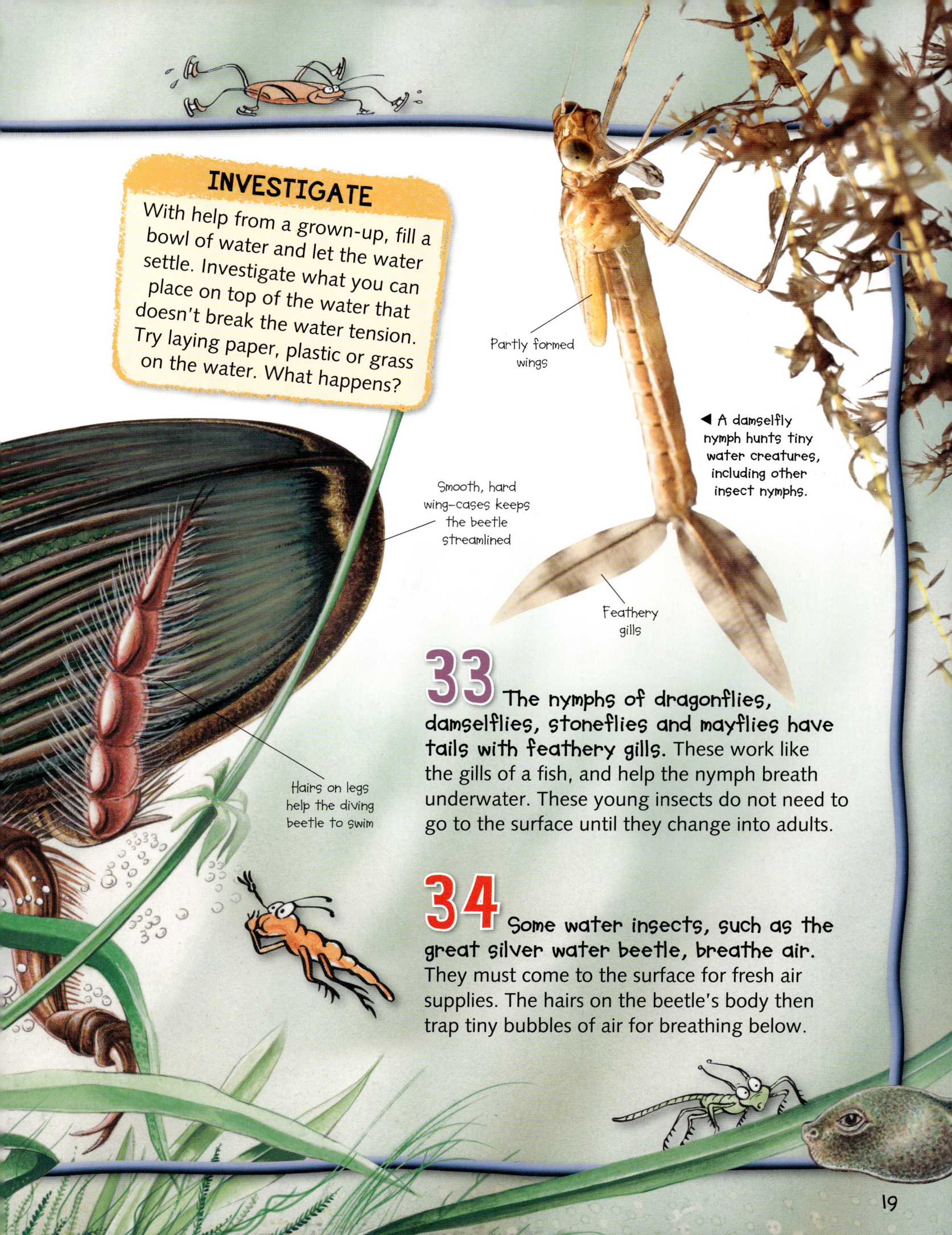

Partly formed wings

Smooth, hard wing-cases keeps the beetle streamlined

◀ A damselfly nymph hunts tiny water creatures, including other insect nymphs.

Feathery gills

Hairs on legs help the diving beetle to swim

33 The nymphs of dragonflies, damselflies, stoneflies and mayflies have tails with feathery gills. These work like the gills of a fish, and help the nymph breath underwater. These young insects do not need to go to the surface until they change into adults.

34 Some water insects, such as the great silver water beetle, breathe air. They must come to the surface for fresh air supplies. The hairs on the beetle's body then trap tiny bubbles of air for breathing below.

Brilliant burrowers

35 **Soil teems with millions of creatures — and many are insects.** Some are larvae or grubs, others are fully-grown insects, such as burrowing beetles, ants, termites and earwigs. These soil insects are a vital source of food for all kinds of larger animals, from spiders and shrews to moles and birds.

36 **The larva of the click beetle is shiny orange, up to 25 millimetres long and called a wireworm.** It stays undergound, feeding on plant parts, for up to five years. Then it changes into an adult and leaves the soil. Wireworms can be serious pests of crops such as barley, oats, wheat, potatoes and beet.

▶ Many insects pose a threat to farmers' crops. Farmers can use pesticides — chemicals to kill the insects — but many people think that this harms other plants and animals.

37 The larva of the cranefly ('daddy longlegs') is called a leatherjacket because of its tough, leathery skin. Leatherjackets eat the roots of grasses, including cereal crops, such as wheat. They hatch from their eggs in late summer and feed in the soil. They change into pupae and then adults the following summer.

INSECT LARVAE
1. African fruit beetle larva
2. Black cutworm caterpillar
3. Cicada grub
4. Click beetle larva
5. Cockchafer grub
6. Leatherjacket
7. Japanese beetle larva

ADULT INSECTS
1. African fruit beetle
2. Black cutworm moth
3. Cicada
4. Click beetle
5. Cockchafer
6. Cranefly
7. Japanese beetle

38 The larva of the cicada may live underground for more than ten years. Different types of cicadas stay in the soil for different periods of time. The American periodic cicada is probably the record holder, taking 17 years to change into a pupa and then an adult. Adults make loud chirping or buzzing sounds.

▶ Adult cicadas suck the sap of bushes and trees.

Bloodthirsty bugs

39 Although most insects are small, they are among the fiercest hunters in the animal world. Many have huge mouthparts shaped like spears or saws, for grabbing and tearing up victims. Some actively chase after prey, while others lie in wait and surprise it.

Powerful jaws for digging and cutting up food

▲ Insect jaws, or mandibles, like this wasp's, move from side-to-side.

40 The antlion larva digs small pits in sand or loose soil. It hides below the surface at the bottom of the pit and waits for small creatures to wander past and slip in. The larva then grasps them with its fang-like mouthparts.

41 The lacewing looks delicate and dainty, but it is a fearsome hunter. It hunts aphids such as greenfly and blackfly, and drinks their body fluids. It may also have a sip of sweet, sugary nectar from a flower.

▼ The lacewing is green to blend in with the leaves where it hunts.

BUGS

42 One of the most powerful insect predators is the praying mantis. It gets its name from the way it holds its front legs folded, like a person with hands together in prayer. The front legs have sharp spines, and snap together like spiky scissors to grab prey, such as moths or caterpillars.

◀ The mantis stays perfectly still, camouflaged by its body colouring, which blends in with the leaf or flower where it waits. When a victim comes near — SNAP!

QUIZ

1. What does a wasp use its jaws for?
2. Finish the name of this insect: praying...?
3. Which insect's larva digs small pits in sand?

Answers:
1. Digging and cutting up food 2. Mantis 3. Antlion

Veggie bugs

◀ Mealybugs, scale insects and aphids can be serious pests in vegetable fields, orchards and greenhouses.

▲ Most shield bugs feed on plant sap using their sucking mouth parts.

43 **About nine out of ten kinds of insects eat some kind of plant food.** Many feed on soft, rich, nutritious substances. These include the sap in stems and leaves, the mineral-rich liquid in roots, the nectar in flowers and the soft flesh of squashy fruits and berries.

44 **Solid wood may not seem very tasty, but many kinds of insects eat it.** They usually consume the wood when they are larvae or grubs, making tunnels as they eat their way through trees, logs and timber structures, such as bridges, fences, houses and furniture.

▶ Woodworms are various kinds of wood-eating beetle larvae. Some stay in the wood for three years or more.

BUGS

45 **Animal droppings are delicious to many kinds of insects.** Various types of beetles lay their eggs in warm, steamy piles of droppings. When the larvae hatch out, they eat the dung.

▲ Dung beetles mould soft dung into a ball shape. They roll the ball into a hole, which they have dug to lay their eggs in. The ball then covers their eggs.

◀ A lacebug jabs its sharp mouthparts into a plant to suck up the rich, syrupy sap inside.

46 **Insects are not fussy eaters!** They feed on old bits of damp and crumbling wood, dying trees, brown and decaying leaves and smelly, rotting fruit. This is nature's way of recycling goodness and nutrients in old plant parts, and returning them to the soil so new trees and other plants can grow.

▲ Fruitworms are insect larvae that may be moth caterpillars or beetle grubs, as shown here.

25

Stings and things

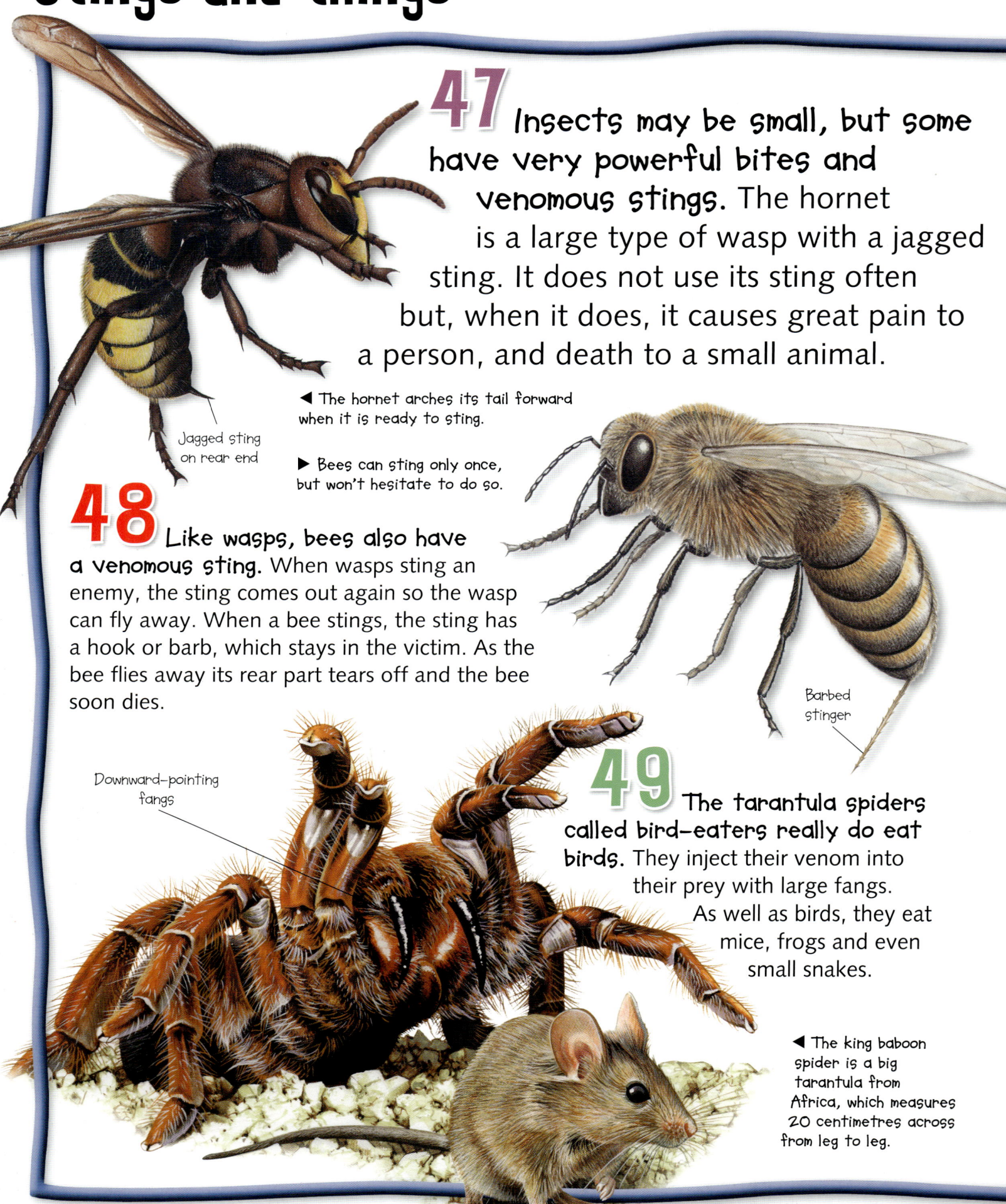

47 **Insects may be small, but some have very powerful bites and venomous stings.** The hornet is a large type of wasp with a jagged sting. It does not use its sting often but, when it does, it causes great pain to a person, and death to a small animal.

◀ The hornet arches its tail forward when it is ready to sting.

Jagged sting on rear end

▶ Bees can sting only once, but won't hesitate to do so.

48 **Like wasps, bees also have a venomous sting.** When wasps sting an enemy, the sting comes out again so the wasp can fly away. When a bee stings, the sting has a hook or barb, which stays in the victim. As the bee flies away its rear part tears off and the bee soon dies.

Barbed stinger

Downward-pointing fangs

49 **The tarantula spiders called bird-eaters really do eat birds.** They inject their venom into their prey with large fangs. As well as birds, they eat mice, frogs and even small snakes.

◀ The king baboon spider is a big tarantula from Africa, which measures 20 centimetres across from leg to leg.

BUGS

QUIZ

1. What happens to a bee when it uses its sting?
2. Do bird-eating spiders really eat birds?
3. What does the bombardier beetle do to avoid attacks?

Answers:
1. It dies 2. Yes 3. It sprays hot liquid at its attacker

50 **To startle and sting an attacker, the bombardier beetle squirts out a spray of hot liquid.** It comes out of its rear end like a spray gun and gives the beetle time to escape.

▼ Army ants march and feed by day, then gather in a clump-like 'living nest' or bivouac to rest at night.

51 **One army ant can give a small bite, but 10,000 ants are much more dangerous.** Army ants are mainly from South America and do not stay in a nest like other ants. They march in long lines through the forest, eating whatever they can bite, sting and overpower, from large spiders to lizards and birds.

Clever colonies

52 Some insects live together in huge groups called colonies, which are like insect cities. There are four main types of insects that form colonies. One is the termites. The other three are all in the same insect subgroup and are bees, wasps and ants.

▶ An ants' nest is packed with tunnels and chambers.

53 Different kinds of ants make nests from whatever material is available. Ants might use mud, small sticks and twigs, tiny bits of stone and gravel, or chewed-up pieces of leaves and flowers.

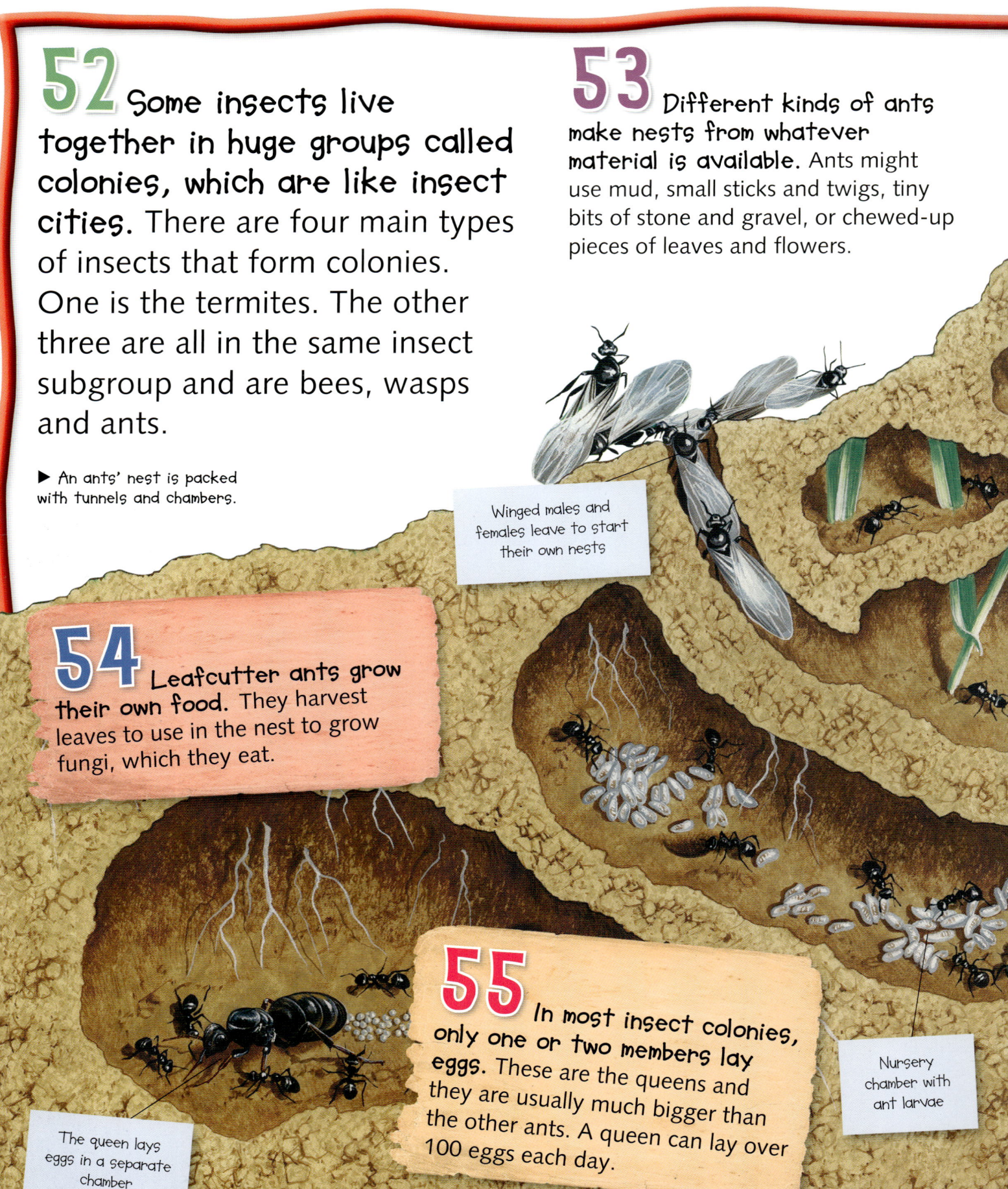

Winged males and females leave to start their own nests

54 Leafcutter ants grow their own food. They harvest leaves to use in the nest to grow fungi, which they eat.

55 In most insect colonies, only one or two members lay eggs. These are the queens and they are usually much bigger than the other ants. A queen can lay over 100 eggs each day.

Nursery chamber with ant larvae

The queen lays eggs in a separate chamber

BUGS

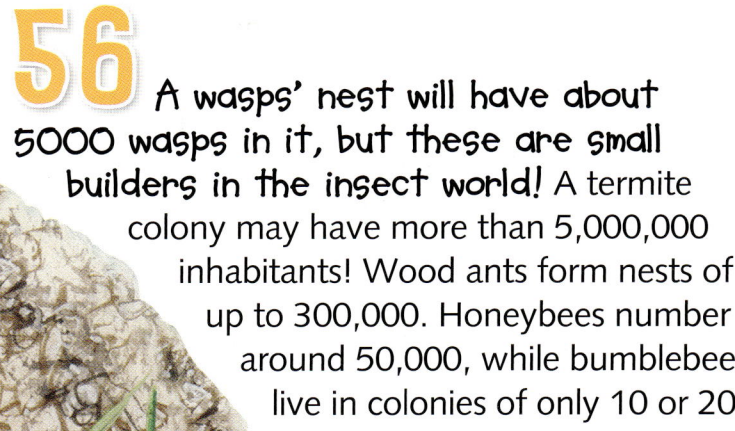
▼ This wasp is making new cells for larvae.

56 A wasps' nest will have about 5000 wasps in it, but these are small builders in the insect world! A termite colony may have more than 5,000,000 inhabitants! Wood ants form nests of up to 300,000. Honeybees number around 50,000, while bumblebees live in colonies of only 10 or 20.

I DON'T BELIEVE IT!
Ants look after aphids and milk them like cows! They stroke the aphids to obtain a sugary liquid called honeydew, which the ants sip to get energy.

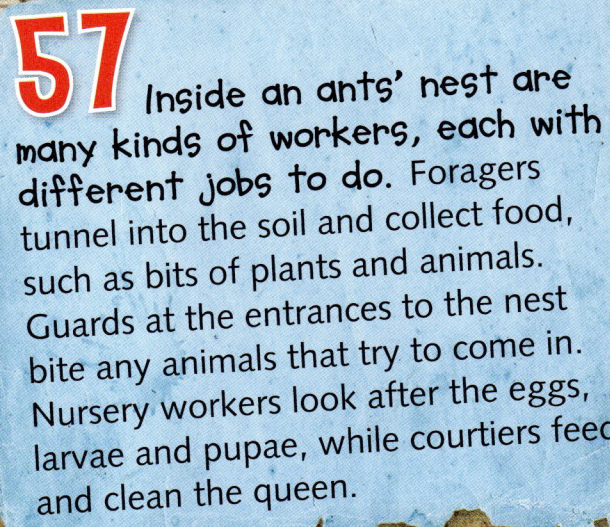

Worker ants care for the eggs and larvae

57 Inside an ants' nest are many kinds of workers, each with different jobs to do. Foragers tunnel into the soil and collect food, such as bits of plants and animals. Guards at the entrances to the nest bite any animals that try to come in. Nursery workers look after the eggs, larvae and pupae, while courtiers feed and clean the queen.

Where am I?

58 Insects have some of the best types of camouflage in the world. Camouflage is when a living thing blends in with its surroundings, so it is difficult to notice. This makes it hard for predators to see it. Or, if the insect is a predator, camouflage helps it to stalk its prey unnoticed.

59 The thornbug has a hard, pointed body casing. It sits still on a twig pretending to be a real thorn. It moves about and feeds at night.

▲ Thornbugs stay completely still during the daytime.

The 'thorn' is part of the thorax

60 Shieldbugs have broad, flat bodies that look like leaves. The body is shaped like a shield carried by a medieval knight-in-armour.

◀ Shieldbugs stay on leaves of their own colour.

BUGS

Abdomen

Thorax

Real stick

Antenna (feeler)

▲ Every part of a stick insect looks stick-like, making it difficult to see what is what!

61 The bird-dropping caterpillar looks just like a pile of bird's droppings! Not many animals would want to eat it, so it survives longer.

▼ The bird-dropping caterpillar is shiny, like new, moist bird dung.

62 Stick and leaf insects look exactly like sticks and leaves. The body and legs are long and twig-like. The body of a leaf insect has wide, flat parts that are coloured to resemble leaves. Both these types of insects eat plants. When the wind blows they rock and sway in the breeze, just like real twigs and leaves.

CREATE CAMOUFLAGE

Colour two pieces of paper with lots of patterns and patches – use the same colours for both bits of paper. Ask a grown-up to help you cut a butterfly shape out of one of the pieces of paper. Lay your butterfly on the other piece of paper – can you see it?

▼ Kallima butterflies look just like leaves when their wings are closed.

63 Many butterflies seem too brightly coloured to blend in with their surroundings. But when the wings are held together over the butterfly's back, the undersides show. These are usually brown or green – dark colours like the leaves.

31

Great pretenders

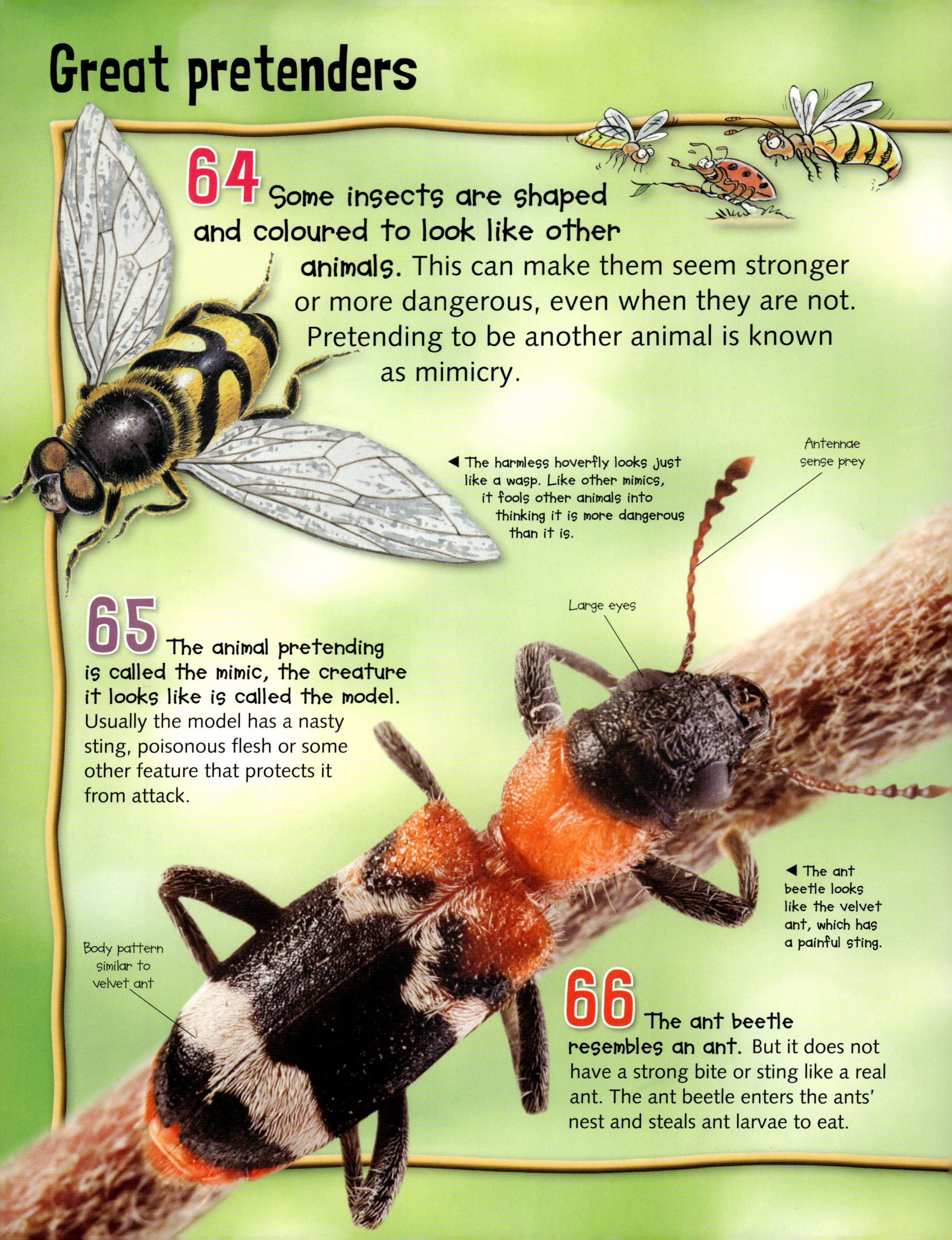

64 Some insects are shaped and coloured to look like other animals. This can make them seem stronger or more dangerous, even when they are not. Pretending to be another animal is known as mimicry.

◀ The harmless hoverfly looks just like a wasp. Like other mimics, it fools other animals into thinking it is more dangerous than it is.

65 The animal pretending is called the mimic, the creature it looks like is called the model. Usually the model has a nasty sting, poisonous flesh or some other feature that protects it from attack.

Antennae sense prey

Large eyes

◀ The ant beetle looks like the velvet ant, which has a painful sting.

Body pattern similar to velvet ant

66 The ant beetle resembles an ant. But it does not have a strong bite or sting like a real ant. The ant beetle enters the ants' nest and steals ant larvae to eat.

BUGS

Monarch butterfly (model)

Viceroy butterfly (mimic)

67 **The monarch butterfly has bright, bold colours on its wings.** These warn other animals, such as birds and lizards, that its flesh tastes horrible and is poisonous. The viceroy butterfly looks very similar to the monarch, but its flesh is not distasteful.

▲ The viceroy butterfly is a mimic of the monarch butterfly.

▲ Hornet moths have coloured wings, unlike real hornets.

68 **The bee fly looks just like a bee.** It has a hairy, striped body and can hover and hum like a bee, but it can't sting.

▶ The bee fly avoids predators by looking like a bee.

69 **The hornet moth is a mimic of the large type of wasp known as the hornet.** A hornet has a very painful sting and few other creatures dare to try and eat it. The hornet moth is harmless, but few other creatures dare to eat it either.

QUIZ

1. Can the bee fly sting?
2. Which butterfly looks similar to the monarch butterfly?
3. Which insect does a hoverfly look like?

Answers:
1. No 2. Viceroy butterfly 3. Wasp

Stay or go?

70 The cold of winter or the dryness of drought mean hard times for most animals, including insects. One way to survive is to hibernate. Many insects find a safe, sheltered place and go to sleep because they are too cold to move. Butterflies crawl behind creepers and vines. Ladybirds cluster in thick bushes. Beetles dig into the soil or among tree roots. As the weather becomes warmer, they become active again.

▼ Ladybirds gather in jumbled piles for winter.

71 In North America, monarch butterflies fly south during autumn. They migrate to warmer areas and millions of them gather in winter roosts. Next spring they all fly north again to feed and breed.

BUGS

72 Some insects migrate the wrong way! In Australia, bogong moths sometimes fly off in search of better conditions. Some keep on flying over the sea, fall into the water and die.

73 Some insects migrate only when they become too numerous. After a few years of good conditions in Africa, locusts (a type of large grasshopper) increase in number so much they form vast swarms. With so many locusts together, they eat all the food in a whole area then fly off to look for more. They eat massive areas of farm crops and people are left to starve.

▲ Some locust swarms are so vast, with billions of insects, they take several days to fly past.

QUIZ

1. How do ladybirds keep warm in winter?
2. How many locusts can be in a swarm?
3. Why do some insects migrate long distances?

Answers:
1. Cluster in bushes 2. Billions 3. To find better conditions to help them survive

Noisy neighbours

74 The tropical forest is warm and still — but far from quiet. Many insects are making chirps, buzzes, clicks, screeches, hums and other noises. Most are males, making their songs or calls to attract females at breeding time.

▶ Katydids, or bush crickets, have loud mating calls.

Labels: Large eye, Chewing mouthparts, Large wings

QUIZ

1. What noise does a cicada make?
2. How does the katydid make noise?
3. Why does a mole cricket dig a burrow?

Answers:
1. Buzzing sound 2. It rubs its wings together 3. To make its chirps louder

BUGS

75 **Some of the noisiest insects are cicadas, plant-eating bugs with large wings.** The male cicada has two thin patches of body casing, called tymbals, one on either side of its abdomen (its rear body part). Tiny muscles pull in each patch, then let it go again, like clicking a tin lid in and out.

Tymbal (sound-making patch)
Air cavity (makes sounds louder)
Tymbal muscle
Compound eyes
Thorax

▶ A cicada's clicks are so fast, they merge into a buzzing sound, which can be heard one kilometre away.

76 **The male mole cricket chirps like a katydid.** It sits at the entrance to its burrow in the soil. The entrance is shaped like a loudspeaker, so it makes the chirps sound louder and travel further.

▶ The mole cricket's song is heard 2 kilometres away.

77 **Like most other crickets, the male katydid chirps by rubbing its wings together.** The bases of the wings near the body have hard, ridged strips like rows of pegs. These click past each other to make the chirping sound.

Meet the family!

78 Are all minibeasts and bugs truly insects? One way to tell is to count the legs. If a creature has six legs, it's an insect. If it has more legs or fewer, it is some other kind of animal. Leg-counting works only with adult creatures.

QUIZ

1. How many legs does an insect have?
2. Is a woodlouse an insect or crustacean?
3. Which has more legs – a millipede or a centipede?

Answers:
1. Six 2. Crustacean 3. Millipede

Single left and right wings

Hard forewing cases called elytra

▶ Flies are insects with six legs and one set of wings.

Flying hindwings folded up under elytra

▲ The cardinal beetle is an insect with six legs and two sets of wings.

▼ The red spider mite has eight legs, like its cousins, the spiders.

Furry body

Feelers and mouthparts

79 Mites and ticks have eight legs, so they are not insects. Ticks, and some mites, cling onto larger animals and suck their blood. Some mites are so small that a handful of soil may contain half a million of them. Mites and ticks belong to the group of animals with eight legs, called arachnids. Other arachnids are spiders and scorpions.

BUGS

▲ Most woodlice have seven pairs of walking legs.

80 A woodlouse has a hard body casing and feelers on its head. It has more than ten legs so it is certainly not an insect! It is a crustacean – a cousin of crabs and lobsters.

81 Millipedes have 50 or 100 legs, maybe even more. They are definitely not insects. Millipedes eat bits of plants, such as old leaves, bark and wood.

Hard ring-like segment

▲ A millipede has four legs on each body segment (section).

Long front fangs

▶ A centipede has two legs on each body segment.

Extra long legs on last segment

82 A centipede has lots of legs, far more than six – usually over 30. It has two very long fangs, which gives it a venomous bite. It races across the ground hunting for insects to eat.

39

Friends and foes

83 Some insects are harmful – but others are very helpful. They are a vital part of the natural world. Flies, butterflies, beetles and many other insects visit flowers to collect nectar and pollen to eat. In the process they carry pollen from flower to flower. This is called pollination and is needed so that the flower can form seeds or fruits.

Bee jaws chew and shape the wax cell walls

Bees communicate by antenna-stroking

84 Bees make honey from flower pollen and nectar. Honey is packed with energy, and bees use it to feed their larvae when conditions are bad. Their visits to flowers pollinate hundreds of kinds of our own food plants. People keep honeybees in hives so the honey is easier to collect.

◀ Honeybees store honey in six-sided compartments called cells, in layers known as honeycombs.

BUGS

85 A few kinds of insects are among the most harmful creatures in the world. They do not attack and kill people directly, like tigers and crocodiles, but they do spread dangerous diseases, such as malaria.

86 Mosquitoes spread diseases by blood-sucking. Their blood-filled bodies are also food for a huge range of animals, from dragonflies and centipedes to frogs, small birds and shrews.

▶ A mosquito sucks blood from human skin.

87 Most insects die from cold and lack of food in the winter. Before they die, they lay tiny eggs in sheltered places. Next year the eggs hatch and the yearly cycle of insect life begins again.

Abdomen held clear of skin

Antennae detect skin warmth

Needle-like mouthparts in skin

88 Spiders are very helpful to gardeners. They catch lots of insect pests, such as flies, in their webs.

89 Insects are so numerous and varied, they provide essential links to the food chains of almost every habitat. Countless small creatures eat insects who have eaten plants, then bigger animals eat the small creatures and so on. If insects disappeared, most other animal life would soon starve!

▲ Spiders play a vital role in our ecosystem.

SPIDERS

90 Spiders may be small, but they are fast-moving, ferocious hunters. These eight-legged mini-beasts inspire fear in many people, but most of them are harmless to humans. Spiders are important predators of flies and other pests. They are also food for other animals, especially birds and insects.

▶ Zoom in close to a tropical wolf spider feeding on a centipede! Spiders are not just creepy-crawlies — they are fascinating creatures with an incredible way of life.

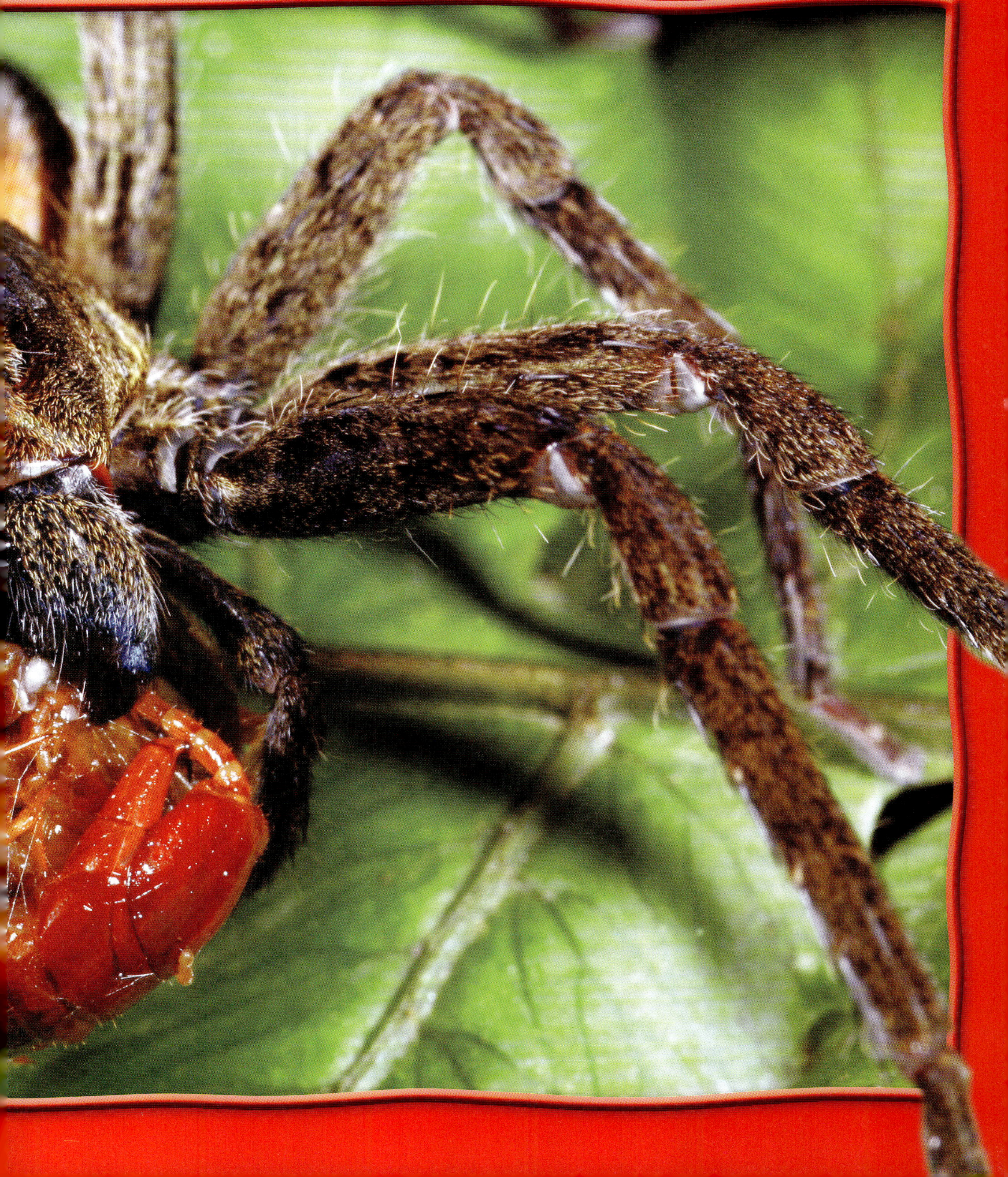

What is a spider?

91 Spiders belong to a group of animals called arachnids. They have eight legs unlike insects, which have six. Almost all spiders live on land and are predators – they hunt other animals to eat.

▼ Like many animals, spiders have organs inside their bodies. The organs carry out essential jobs, such as digesting food and circulating blood.

TRUE OR FALSE?
1. Spiders are insects.
2. Predators are animals that eat grass.
3. A spider's palps inject venom into prey.

Answers:
All are false

92 A spider's body is divided into two parts, which are connected by a slender stalk. The front part of the body is called a cephalothorax (say: kef-a-low-thor-ax) and the rear part is called the abdomen.

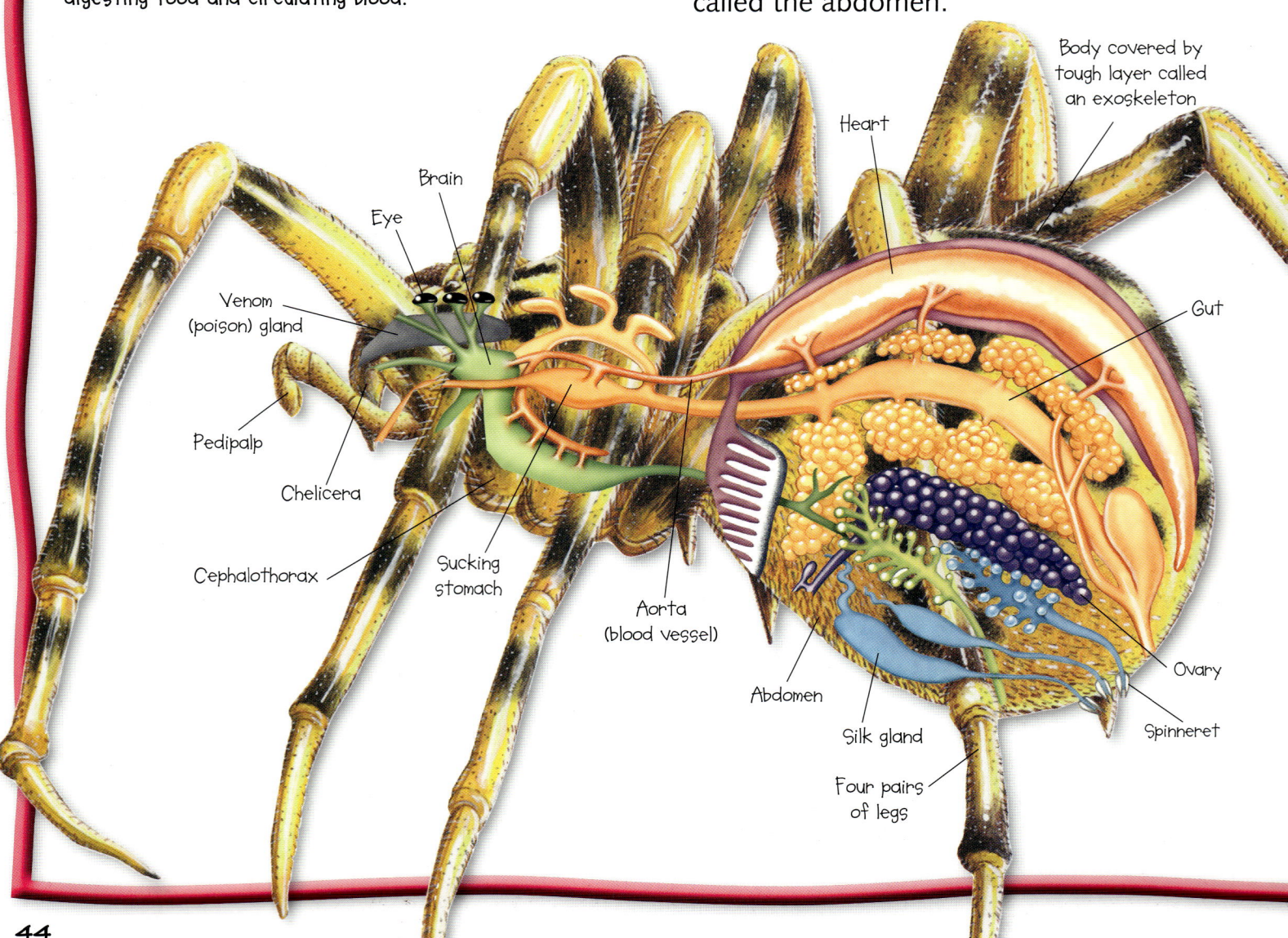

Labels: Brain, Eye, Venom (poison) gland, Pedipalp, Chelicera, Cephalothorax, Sucking stomach, Aorta (blood vessel), Abdomen, Silk gland, Four pairs of legs, Heart, Body covered by tough layer called an exoskeleton, Gut, Ovary, Spinneret

SPIDERS

▲ Garden spiders have large, swollen abdomens. The small, black eyes are visible at the front of the head.

▲ These common arachnids have three pairs of spinnerets at the tips of their abdomens.

93 Spiders can make threads of super-strong silk. They can build with it, throw it and wind it. Because spiders can make silk, they have been able to survive in most land habitats. One type of spider even uses its silk to live underwater.

94 Pedipalps, chelicerae and spinnerets are useful tools for spiders. Leg-like pedipalps are short feelers, fangs in the chelicerae inject deadly venom (poison) into prey, and spinnerets produce silk to wrap prey up.

95 About 40,000 species (types) of spiders have been named so far. There are plenty more waiting to be discovered. These animals walked our planet long before the dinosaurs and have been around for at least 300 million years.

45

Shapes and sizes

96 Almost every spider in the world is smaller than your hand. Most of them are even smaller than your little finger. However, there are some giants and midgets in the arachnid family – and some spiders that don't even look like spiders!

MAKING SPIDERS

You will need:
scissors   egg carton
pipe cleaners   coloured pens

Cut out each section of an egg carton. Each one will be a spider's body. Poke pipe cleaners through the sides to make the legs. Decorate the body with eyes and markings.

ACTUAL SIZE

97 Goliath bird-eating spiders are enormous, but they don't normally eat birds. Goliaths eat mostly bugs, mice, lizards and frogs. The world's largest spider is the giant huntsman spider. It has a leg span of 30 centimetres, and lives in caves in Laos, in Southeast Asia.

◄ This is the actual size of a goliath bird-eating spider. These spiders are too big to climb easily, so they mostly live on the ground in burrows.

98 Crab spiders look and move just like crabs. The females have large, round bodies, and they can scuttle backwards or sideways when scared. Some crab spiders have pointed humps on their abdomens and little horns on their heads.

▲ Female spiders are often bigger than males. This is especially true of crab spiders. The females are often more colourful too.

99 Not all spiders have a round body and long legs. Ant spiders look just like weaver ants, and peacock spiders have beautiful colours more often seen in birds. The bird dung spider has the best disguise – it looks like bird poo!

▼ A male peacock spider raises its body and legs to show off its beautiful colours.

◀ Spiny orb weavers are often boldly coloured, and have spines or horns on their bodies.

100 Midget spiders are the smallest spiders in the world. Their bodies are usually no more than 5 millimetres long. One male found on the island of Western Samoa measured just 0.43 millimetres – smaller than a pinhead. Their webs can be less than 10 millimetres across.

Fearsome family

101 **Spiders have some fearsome relatives.** Scorpions, ticks and mites all belong to the arachnid family. Other less fearsome family members are false scorpions, harvestmen and sun-spiders.

102 **Scorpions are the oldest of all arachnids.** Fossils show that some scorpions have reached lengths of nearly 90 centimetres. Larger species are usually less venomous than smaller ones. The most dangerous species is the death-stalker scorpion.

▲ Scorpions have large pincers and nasty stings in their tails.

▶ There are different types or 'orders' of animals in the Arachnid class.

CLASS: *Arachnida*

- ORDER: *Areneida* Spiders
- ORDER: *Scorpiones* Scorpions
- ORDER: *Parasitiformes* Ticks and mites
- ORDER: *Opilones* Harvestmen
- ORDER: *Solpugida* Sun-spiders

103 **Ticks and mites are tiny arachnids that can survive in almost every land habitat.** Miniature mites are not even one millimetre long, and most live and feed on other animals and plants. Many types of ticks are pests that suck the blood of animals and humans, spreading disease.

▼ When ticks start to drink blood, their soft bodies stretch as they swell, so there is space for more.

◀ Tiny red velvet mites are often found in gardens. They live in soil and feed on insects.

SPIDERS

104 Scientists are hoping to use scorpion venom to cure all kinds of medical problems. Chinese doctors have known for centuries that venom can be used as a powerful painkiller.

105 Sun-spiders have enormous biting chelicerae. However, they don't have venom. They use sucker pads on their pedipalps to hold their prey down, while chewing with their pincer-like chelicerae. Sun-spiders feed on insects and pests, such as termites.

▶ Sun-spiders have ten or 11 segments in their abdomens. The abdomen of a spider has no segments.

▲ Harvestmen are often mistaken for spiders. However, these arachnids have just one rounded body part and not two, like spiders.

106 Harvestmen have small bodies and eight long, skinny legs. They have a cunning trick for survival – if attacked, they shed one of their legs, which continues to move! The predator is distracted by the twitching leg while the harvestman makes a quick getaway on its remaining legs!

Segment

Super spider senses

Jumping spider

Crab spider

Ogre-faced spider

Spitting spider

▲ Spiders with large eyes need to see in the dark or focus on prey.

▼ A male tarantula strokes strands of silk at the entrance to a female's burrow. She senses the movement and comes out.

107 Although spiders have several eyes, they don't rely on their eyesight. Taste, smell and vibration are all important in helping spiders find their way around, locate prey and avoid being eaten!

108 Most spiders have eight eyes, which are arranged in two or three rows at the front of the head. Their main eyes can see images in focus and with detail, while their side eyes spot movement. It is thought that all spiders may be able to see in colour. However, like insects, spiders probably can't see the colour red.

109 Spiders are very hairy! This helps them to hunt, because the tiny hairs are very sensitive to being moved by air and touch. Spiders also have tiny areas, called slit organs, dotted around their exoskeletons. Cave spiders are completely blind, but they can find a fly 30 centimetres away by using the information they get from their hairs and slit organs.

▶ The legs of a Mexican red-knee tarantula are covered with touch-sensitive hairs.

SPIDERS

◀ Jumping spiders use the four large eyes on the front of their heads to see their prey and judge distance when hunting.

TOUCHY-FEELY TEATIME
Ask a grown up to prepare a meal that you can eat using your fingers. Cover your eyes with a blindfold and try to identify the foods using your senses of touch, smell and taste.

110 Spiders don't have tongues and noses — they use their legs to taste and smell! A spider may have as many as 1000 special hairs on each leg that can detect smell and taste. A quick prod will tell a spider if a dead fly is fresh and can be eaten, or old and rotting and should be left alone.

▶ Ogre-faced, or net-casting, spiders have big eyes so they can see at night. They focus on their prey as they throw a silken net over it.

111 Spiders that use their eyes to find prey are often active in the day. They usually hunt and grab their prey. Spiders that rely more on their touch senses are nocturnal, which means they are most active at night. Nocturnal spiders usually catch their prey in silken webs or traps.

Smooth movers

112 **Spiders can run very fast.** The fastest spider ever recorded was a female house spider, covering a distance 330 times her own body length in ten seconds! Spiders can't keep running for long before they become exhausted.

114 **Humans can't run at anywhere near the speed of a spider.** If a human sprinter wanted to run as fast as the world's fastest house spider, they would need to reach speeds of 216 kilometres an hour!

▼ Wolf spiders are all-round athletes! They can walk, stalk, run and even skate on water when they pursue their prey.

113 **Moving eight legs takes a lot of energy and co-ordination, so spiders usually move just four legs at a time.** When a spider walks it might use the first and third leg on its left side, and the second and fourth leg on its right side, while the other four legs rest. The rested legs then take the next step.

115 **Young spiders have little legs, so they take to the skies to move long distances.** They face the wind and throw a silken thread into the air. The wind lifts them up and carries them away – this is called 'ballooning'. Pilots have seen ballooning spiders at heights of several thousand metres!

SPIDERS

◀ The underside of a spider's foot is covered in hairs. Each hair is split into microscopic end-feet.

Tufts of hair, called scopulae
Claw

▲ Claws on the end of a spider's feet help it to grasp silk threads and walk along them.

116 Spiders can walk on smooth surfaces. Their feet, which are called tarsi, are covered with thick tufts of hair. Each hair is divided into thousands of tiny parts, called end-feet. The end-feet stick to walls so well that a spider can raise several feet at once without falling off.

117 Lots of spiders are able to walk on water. Raft spiders use this skill to find food. They rest their front legs on the water's surface to sense vibrations caused by animals beneath. When a fish or tadpole comes close, the raft spider glides over the water and grabs it.

▼ Being able to walk on water has given this raft spider an advantage over land spiders. It has been able to grab a large, juicy stickleback fish to eat.

Spider mates

118 When male spiders are old enough to mate, they often stop eating. They put all their energy into finding a female. Many males die soon after mating.

▼ A male garden spider attaches a special mating thread to the female's web. He taps the thread, and the female comes to investigate.

Female

119 Male spiders perform courtship dances to impress the females. Every species has its own courtship routine, so females can recognize males of their species. Male scaffold web spiders rub part of their carapace (shell-like covering over the cephalothorax) against their abdomen, making a loud noise to call females.

◀ Male jumping spiders raise their legs in a mating display called a courtship.

SPIDERS

120 **Male ornate jumping spiders have clever tricks to attract females.** They position themselves on leaves in full sunlight and begin to dance. Their bodies have special scales that reflect ultraviolet light. The females' eyes detect it as a glow. They walk towards the glow, and the males drum the leaves with their feet, to keep the females' attention.

Male

121 **Female spiders are usually bigger than males.** If a male tries to mate with a female who isn't interested in him, or who has already mated, she may treat him like prey and swiftly bite and eat him.

122 **When two male wolf spiders want to mate with the same female they will fight.** They lift their legs to threaten one another, and the smaller male usually scuttles away. Males sometimes grasp one another with their strong chelicerae.

123 **It is often said that female spiders eat their mates.** However, most males escape unharmed. Some smart male crab spiders wrap the females up in silk before mating, then run away before they break free. Others present their mates with packages of food.

Spiderlings

124 Female spiders wrap their eggs in a silken cocoon. Each cocoon may contain just two eggs, but some species lay 2000 eggs at a time! The smallest eggs are almost impossible to see, while the largest ones are the size of a pea.

125 While some mothers leave their eggs after laying them, others take special care of their brood. Nursery-web spiders carry their eggs around until they find a good place to hang the egg-sac.

Tent-like web protects the freshly hatched spiderlings

▲ Spiders build a silken cocoon when they are ready to lay their eggs. Some lay more than 1000 eggs in just ten minutes.

◀ Female nursery-web spiders build a tent-like web to protect their eggs.

Female nursery-web spider guarding her nest

WATCH YOURSELF GROW
Spiders moult to grow bigger, but humans grow more gradually. Discover your weight and height. Make a chart to record how they change over a period of six months or one year.

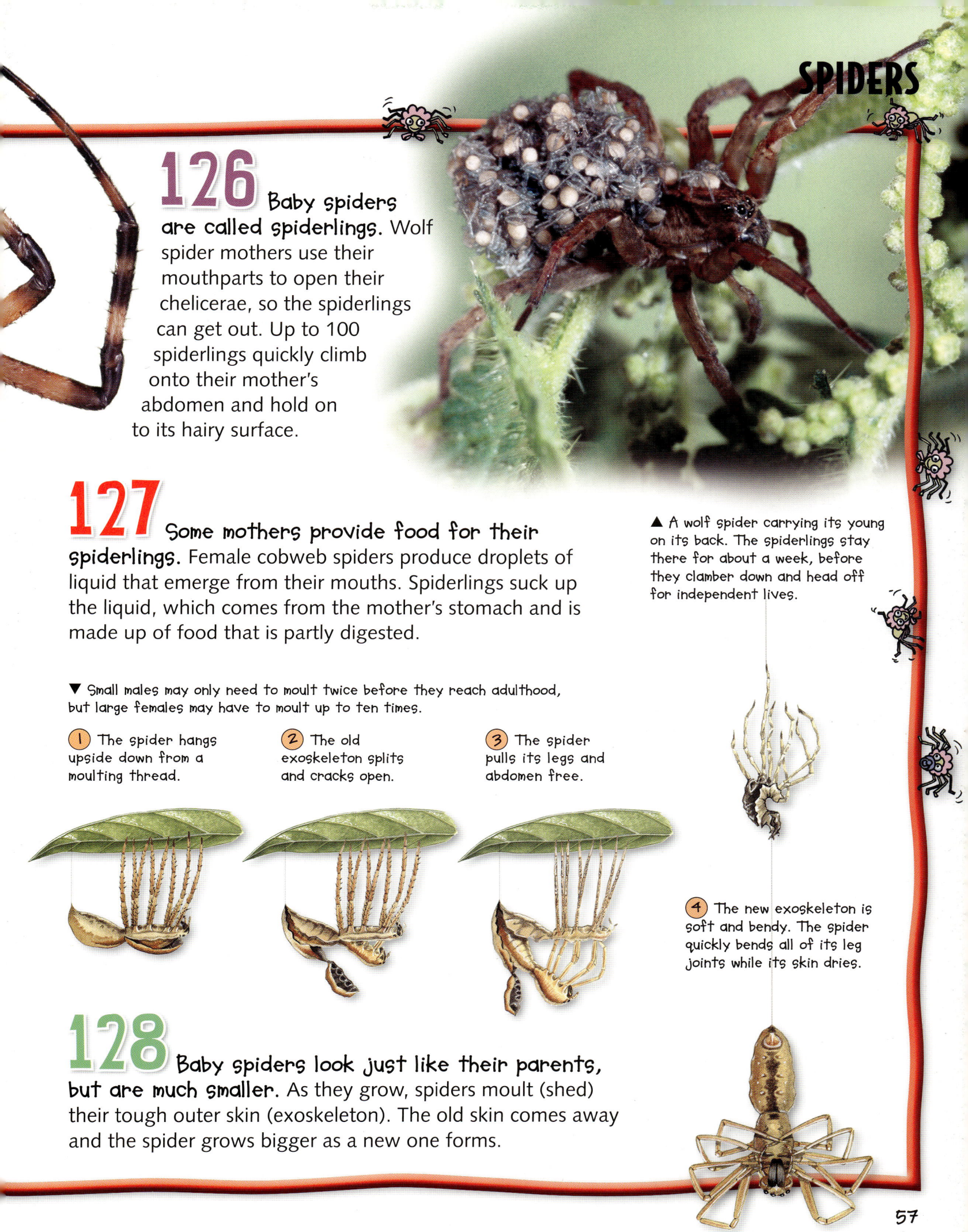

SPIDERS

126 Baby spiders are called spiderlings. Wolf spider mothers use their mouthparts to open their chelicerae, so the spiderlings can get out. Up to 100 spiderlings quickly climb onto their mother's abdomen and hold on to its hairy surface.

▲ A wolf spider carrying its young on its back. The spiderlings stay there for about a week, before they clamber down and head off for independent lives.

127 Some mothers provide food for their spiderlings. Female cobweb spiders produce droplets of liquid that emerge from their mouths. Spiderlings suck up the liquid, which comes from the mother's stomach and is made up of food that is partly digested.

▼ Small males may only need to moult twice before they reach adulthood, but large females may have to moult up to ten times.

① The spider hangs upside down from a moulting thread.

② The old exoskeleton splits and cracks open.

③ The spider pulls its legs and abdomen free.

④ The new exoskeleton is soft and bendy. The spider quickly bends all of its leg joints while its skin dries.

128 Baby spiders look just like their parents, but are much smaller. As they grow, spiders moult (shed) their tough outer skin (exoskeleton). The old skin comes away and the spider grows bigger as a new one forms.

Where spiders live

129 There are spiders in the Arctic, in deserts, by the sea and even on top of mountains. They are most common in places where there are lots of plants. Spiders live under stones and plants, and in fields, farms, forests and buildings.

▼ Beach wolf spiders blend in with their sandy homes. Patterns on their skin help them to hide from predators.

▲ Adult cave spiders hide from light. When their spiderlings hatch from a cocoon, they find new homes by running towards light.

130 Spiders living in cool places find it hard to survive the winter. The cold and shortage of food means that few of these species are active during the coldest times of year. Some of them dig into leaf litter and rest, or hibernate, until spring. Others lay their eggs before winter and die, and the eggs then hatch in spring.

I DON'T BELIEVE IT!
Young water spiders can't spin themselves a silken home, so they take over empty pond snail shells and fill them with air to breathe.

SPIDERS

131 **Most spiders live alone, but there are a few friendly types.** Lynx spiders live in warm tropical rainforests and work together to build large webs. The groups, or colonies, contain hundreds of spiders, including males, females and spiderlings.

132 **There is only one type of spider in the world that can live in water.** It can be difficult for air-breathing animals to live underwater. The water spider traps bubbles of air from the surface and takes them to its underwater web. It mates, lays eggs and eats its prey inside the waterproof silken structure.

▲ Spiders that live and work together are called social spiders. This way of life is rare for arachnids.

133 **In 1924 an explorer found spiders living at a height of 6700 metres on Mount Everest.** The spiders were sheltering from the extreme weather by hiding under stones. It is thought these spiders survive by eating food carried up the mountain by the wind.

▶ A water spider carries a bubble of air underwater. It will use the bubble to top up the air supplies inside its silken home, which is called a retreat.

Super silk

◀ A grasshopper is caught inside a web of super-strong silk. The spider keeps wrapping the silk around the insect's body to make a neat little package.

134 All spiders are able to make silk. The silken threads are made of protein and produced in special silk glands. Its unique qualities make it one of the most incredible substances on Earth.

135 Scientists would love to unravel silk's many secrets. No fibres made by humans can match silk's strength and elasticity (stretchiness). It can stretch up to six times its length before snapping. Silk could be used to make ultra-tough fabric for sportspeople or people who work in dangerous places. If a 20-millimetre-thick fibre of silk could be made, it could lift a truck.

SPIDERS

QUIZ

1. What are a spider's silken threads made of?
2. Where are they produced?
3. What do weaver ants use their larvae's silk for?

Answers:
1. Protein 2. In special silk glands 3. To build huge nests

136 **Spiders can make different kinds of silk.** Some threads are dry but extremely strong, while other kinds are moist and elastic. Spiders use different silk for different jobs, such as making webs or cocoons to protect their eggs.

137 **Spiders are not the only animals that can make silk.** Adult weaver ants use their larvae as silk-making machines! These insects use leaves to make nests at the tops of trees. When they need to bind the leaves together, the ants grab their larvae and move them from side to side. The silk that the larvae produce hold the leaf edges together.

138 **Spider silk is coated in a sticky 'glue'.** Scientists have been trying to find a way to copy this 'glue', because it is very strong. It could possibly be made from cheaper, more environmentally friendly ingredients than other glues (which are often made from oil).

▲ Green tree ants are a type of weaver ant. They use their larvae's silk to build huge nests.

▼ Butterfly and moth larvae also make silk. Spindle ermine moth larvae have covered this tree with silken webs.

Weaving and building

139 Spiders use their strong silken threads for many things. Silk is used to make draglines to travel, to protect eggs, to hide from predators and to wrap up prey. Many spiders also use silk to build traps and webs.

140 Silk glands inside the abdomen produce liquid silk. It is up to 300,000 times lighter than solid silk. Each gland leads to a spinneret, with an opening called a spigot. When the liquid silk is forced towards the spigot, its tiny particles line up into long fibres and turn solid. The spider's abdomen and spinnerets help the spider direct its threads.

◀ Silken threads are incredibly fine, but they are strong enough to support the weight of a spider.

▲ Silk emerges from an orbweaver's spigot. The spider uses its feet to pull the threads out.

WONDERFUL WEBS

Find several spiders' webs. Use a sketchbook and pencil to copy the patterns and shapes of the webs. Can you see the spiders that built each one?

SPIDERS

141 Some spiders build beautiful, tidy webs that are stretched out like nets. Others make scruffy, disorganized meshes of silk. Daddy longlegs spiders make some of the untidiest webs of all.

▲ Daddy longlegs spiderlings stay in their mother's messy web when they hatch.

142 Spiders that build sheet webs weave flat, silken mats and hide underneath them. Silken threads hang down onto the sheets, and when the spider senses an insect's movement, it shakes its web. The insect falls into the sheet and the spider tears through the web to bite its prey.

143 Spiders recycle their silk. When traps and webs get old they lose their strength and stretchiness. Spiders eat the threads and the silk proteins are reused to make more silk in their silk glands.

▼ A female money spider hangs upside-down below her delicate sheet web. When finished, the sheet will be a dome shape, constructed from ultra-fine threads of silk.

63

On the menu

144 Almost all spiders are carnivores — they eat other animals. They prey on insects or other invertebrates (animals without backbones), especially spiders.

◀ A female green lynx spider has its fangs in a fly. All spiders are equipped with venom, which is a deadly poison that paralyzes victims (stops them from moving). It is injected by fangs on their chelicerae.

SPIDERS

145 Crab spiders prey on large insects, such as butterflies. They don't eat the tough exoskeleton, so the butterfly's remains look almost untouched after the spider has finished its meal.

▲ A gold leaf crab spider bites a hole in a honeybee's body. It then sucks out the insect's insides.

146 Orbweaving spiders trap their prey, bite it, wrap it in silk and wait for it to die. They vomit digestive juices over their prey, turning it to liquid. Then the spiders suck the liquid up. The mouthparts of most spiders are lined with tiny hairs, which act like a filter when sucking up liquid.

147 Only one type of spider is known to be mostly vegetarian. *Bagheera kiplingi* spiders feast on tasty nodules that grow on acacia trees. They sometimes also suck nectar from flowers. However, they do occasionally feed on ant larvae.

QUIZ

1. Is a meat eater called a carnivore or a carnival?
2. Is the tough outer skin of an insect or spider called leather or exoskeleton?
3. If something is nutritious, is it a good food or a poisonous newt?

Answers:
1. A carnivore 2. Exoskeleton 3. A good food

On the run

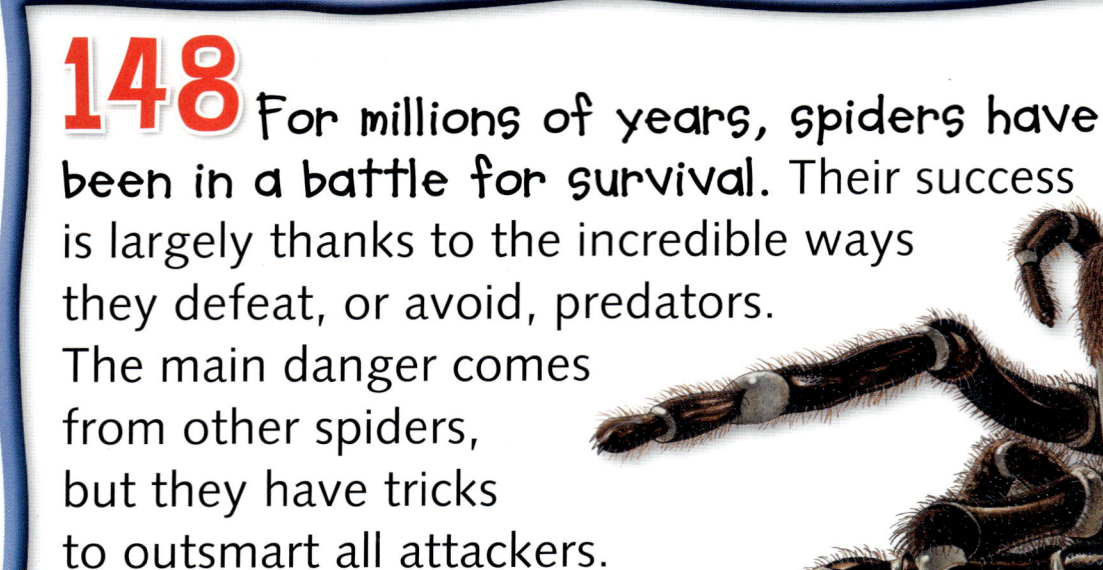

148 For millions of years, spiders have been in a battle for survival. Their success is largely thanks to the incredible ways they defeat, or avoid, predators. The main danger comes from other spiders, but they have tricks to outsmart all attackers.

149 Spiders can run fast or 'fly' to make a quick getaway. They don't have wings, but spiders can throw a lasso of silk, called a dragline, to a nearby plant or twig and swing out of harm's way.

▲ Funnel web spiders look scary when they rear up. They can move fast but they can't jump.

150 Some spiders are masters of arachnobatics! Somersaulting spiders of the Sahara desert can whizz down a sand dune by doing flips and cartwheels. However, spiders can overdo the gymnastics – too many flips and turns can exhaust a spider so much that it dies.

◄ A golden wheel spider rolls down a sand dune to escape a predator. It can reach a top speed of 2 metres per second – that's as fast as a person cartwheeling the length of a football pitch in two seconds!

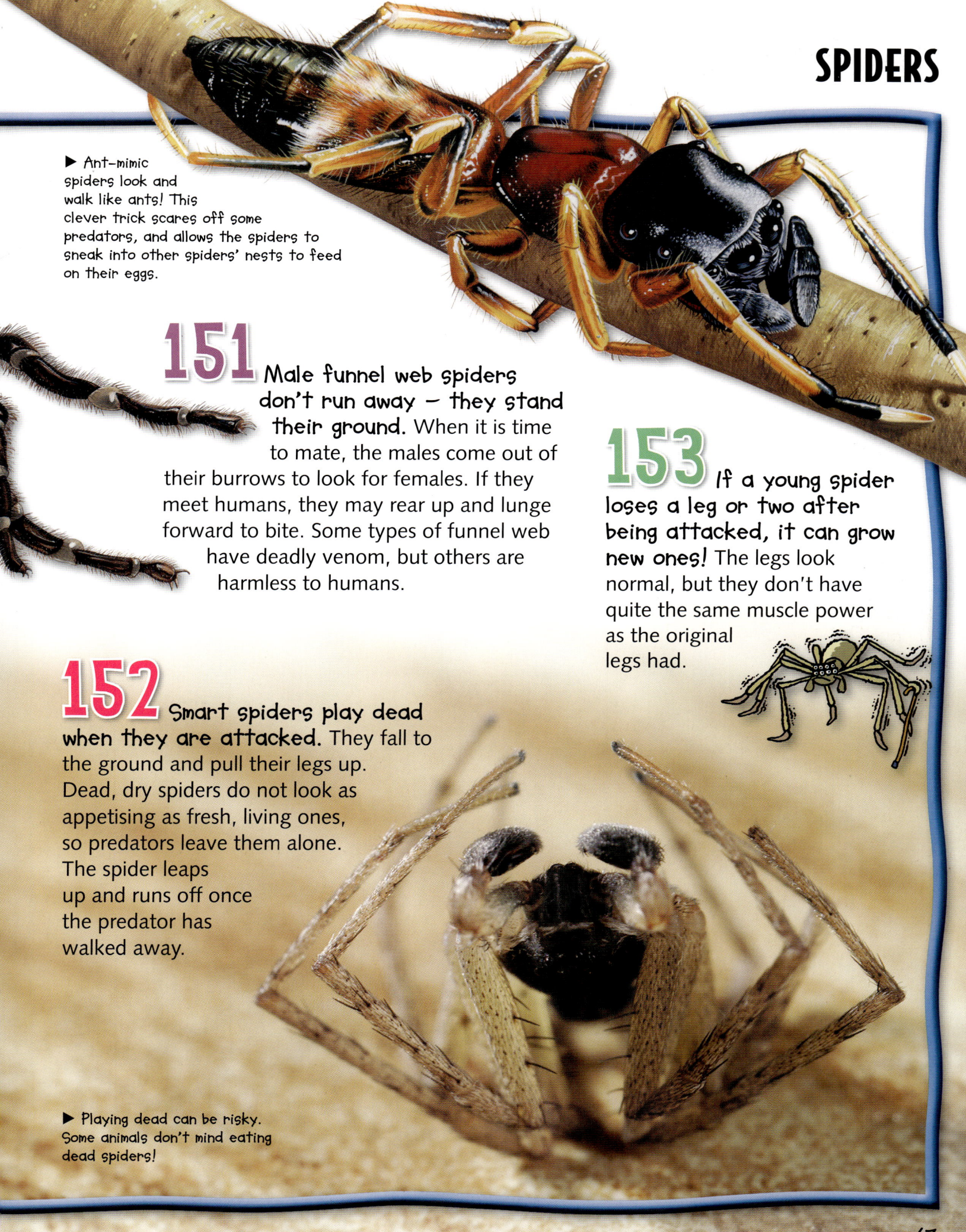

SPIDERS

▶ Ant-mimic spiders look and walk like ants! This clever trick scares off some predators, and allows the spiders to sneak into other spiders' nests to feed on their eggs.

151 **Male funnel web spiders don't run away — they stand their ground.** When it is time to mate, the males come out of their burrows to look for females. If they meet humans, they may rear up and lunge forward to bite. Some types of funnel web have deadly venom, but others are harmless to humans.

153 **If a young spider loses a leg or two after being attacked, it can grow new ones!** The legs look normal, but they don't have quite the same muscle power as the original legs had.

152 **Smart spiders play dead when they are attacked.** They fall to the ground and pull their legs up. Dead, dry spiders do not look as appetising as fresh, living ones, so predators leave them alone. The spider leaps up and runs off once the predator has walked away.

▶ Playing dead can be risky. Some animals don't mind eating dead spiders!

67

Death by stealth

154 Spiders can be divided into two groups — those that hunt their prey and those that catch or trap it. The spiders that hunt their prey are often called 'wandering spiders' and have special skills.

155 Spiders that hunt at night are often dark in colour and covered in lots of fine hairs. Their colour helps them to stay hidden and the hairs, along with their sensory slit organs, help them to detect vibrations caused by other creatures' movement.

◀ Spitting spiders spit a mixture of venom and 'glue' at their prey. They can attack from a distance of 10 millimetres away — nearly twice their body length.

156 Spitting spiders blast a jet of sticky poison at their prey. The lethal liquids are fired at lightning speed, giving the victim no time to escape. The spider can then bite its prey to death and devour its meal.

157 The mouse spider creeps around houses, stealthily stalking prey. During the day these hunters rest in a silken home, hidden from view. At night they search for flies, moths and mosquitoes and leap on them, delivering a deadly bite.

SPIDERS

The trapdoor is disguised with plants and soil

◀ When an unsuspecting bug walks over the trapdoor, the spider leaps out to catch it.

Some burrows have side chambers, where the spider lurks

158 Trapdoor spiders lurk in burrows that are hidden from view. They build a trapdoor that covers the entrance to the burrow, and cover it with plants and soil. The trapdoor is made of silk and the tunnels are lined with silk.

The spider may hide under a flap at the bottom of the hole

160 Brazilian wandering spiders have the largest venom glands of all spiders. They have enough venom to kill 225 mice.

▼ A crab spider's front two pairs of legs are longer and stronger than its other legs. It uses them to reach forward and grab prey.

159 Spiders are perfectly suited to their habitats. Female crab spiders are often coloured to match the flowers they live on, and some types can even change colour. Wandering insects walk right past the spiders, which are almost invisible.

Orb-web spiders

161 Orb-web spiders create the most extraordinary silk structures. They use the least amount of silk necessary to build the largest traps. One spider can weave an entire web in just 30 minutes.

162 When we think of spiders' webs, we usually think of an orb web. However, fewer than 10 percent of spiders build webs like these. Most orb webs are built in the evening or early hours of the morning. They are almost invisible unless dew or rain settles on the strands.

▶ The hardest part of building a web is getting the first thread in place. The spider needs a gust of wind to carry the thread across, so it sticks to a good spot.

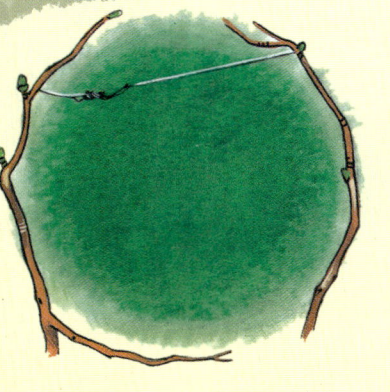

1. The first thread is horizontal
2. The second thread makes a Y-shape 
3. More strands, called radials, are added 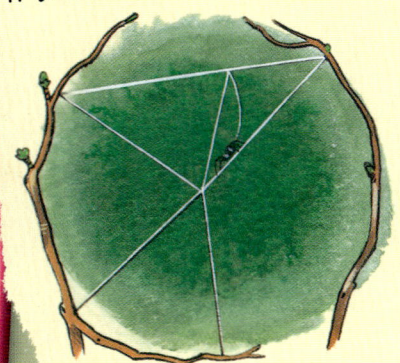
4. A temporary spiral is put in place 
5. The final spiral is built more carefully

SPIDERS

▶ Tiny cucumber spiders can build orb webs between two sides of a leaf.

▲ Early morning dew often destroys webs. Garden spiders have to repair or rebuild their webs almost every day.

164 **The smallest orb webs are built by midget spiders.** These are the smallest spiders in the world. One of their webs may be less than 10 millimetres from one side to the other.

165 **Spiders don't learn how to build webs – they just know how to do it.** In fact, young spiders usually build better, neater webs than older spiders!

163 **Orb weaver spiders build their webs near water, because flying insects often live nearby.** Their brown, velvety bodies are camouflaged against the fences, bridges and buildings where they often set their traps. They are common throughout Europe and North America.

166 **The largest orb webs are built by tropical golden orb-web spiders.** Their threads can measure several metres, and the web itself can measure up to 2 metres wide. The webs are so large they can even trap birds that fly into them!

Funnel web spiders

167 Australian funnel webs are amongst the most dangerous spiders in the world. A single bite can cause a person pain, blindness, difficulty in breathing and sometimes death. Strangely, dogs, cats and rabbits are unaffected by their bite.

▶ Sydney funnel web spiders have huge fangs and deadly venom. Males are more venomous than females.

The fangs inject a venom that causes great pain

Dark body with strong, thick legs

168 Funnel web spiders use untidy silken sheets to create tunnels. They hide at one end of the tunnel and wait for their prey to step onto a flat sheet at its opening. *Tegenaria* are a group of funnel web house spiders. They spin tunnels in dark corners, and are very hairy and extremely fast. They live in Europe and North America.

QUIZ

These spider words have been muddled up. Can you rearrange the letters?

ENMOV
EBBCOW
LINGSPERID
LISK

Answers:
VENOM COBWEB SPIDERLING SILK

SPIDERS

▶ A ladybird larva struggles to escape from a dense web of silken fibres. The movement alerted this labyrinth spider, which has rushed to attack.

169 Labyrinth spiders build enormous silk webs outside their tunnel lairs. The webs are a mass of threads that drape over and between low bushes. Although the threads are not especially sticky, when an insect flies into them, it falls down onto a silken sheet below. The spider can sense the movement instantly, as the threads twitch, and races to the spot where the insect has fallen.

▼ The woodlouse touches the threads, alerting the tube-web spider in its hole.

170 Tube-web spiders don't catch fish, but they do use fishing lines! The spiders hide inside their tunnels, with slender threads of silk stretching out from the entrance. One or two legs rest on the fishing lines, and when they feel movement, they put out more feet to work out exactly where their prey is. They make a last minute dash, grab their prey, give it a venomous bite and return to the tunnel to eat.

73

Widows and wolves

171 The black widow spider has a fearsome reputation, but it is usually timid. These American arachnids often lurk in dark corners of houses where people put their fingers or toes. Disturbing a female black widow might make her bite. Her venom causes great pain and sometimes death.

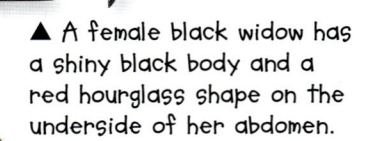

▲ A female black widow has a shiny black body and a red hourglass shape on the underside of her abdomen.

◀ Katipos live in New Zealand, where their name means 'night-stinger'.

172 Black widows belong to a group of arachnids called cobweb or comb-footed spiders. Sticky drops are spread around their messy webs to glue prey in place. Once an insect is trapped, most of the threads around it snap, and the insect springs upwards to be grabbed by the waiting spider.

▲ Australian redbacks belong to the same family as black widows and katipos. They rarely leave their webs, so it is unusual for humans to be bitten.

173 European cobweb spiders build and decorate their homes. They hang silken tubes from their webs, and cover them with bits of plant and soil to disguise them from predators while they rest inside.

▶ European black widow spiders live in hot, dry places. Their bite is painful but not deadly.

SPIDERS

174 Wolf spiders have two large main eyes that help them to see and follow their prey during the day. However, their eyesight is not perfect, and they recognize their prey by the beating of its wings, or the vibrations caused by the way it walks.

▶ Wolf spiders are not as scary as they look. These large, hairy, ground-dwelling hunters prowl around looking for prey, but they are harmless to humans.

175 Male wolf spiders use sign language to tell females they are on the lookout for a mate. They wave their palps around in a special pattern to attract a female's attention and tell her what species they are.

I DON'T BELIEVE IT!
Female Australian redbacks expect males to spend at least 100 minutes 'dancing' before mating can take place. If a male's courtship doesn't impress the female, she eats him!

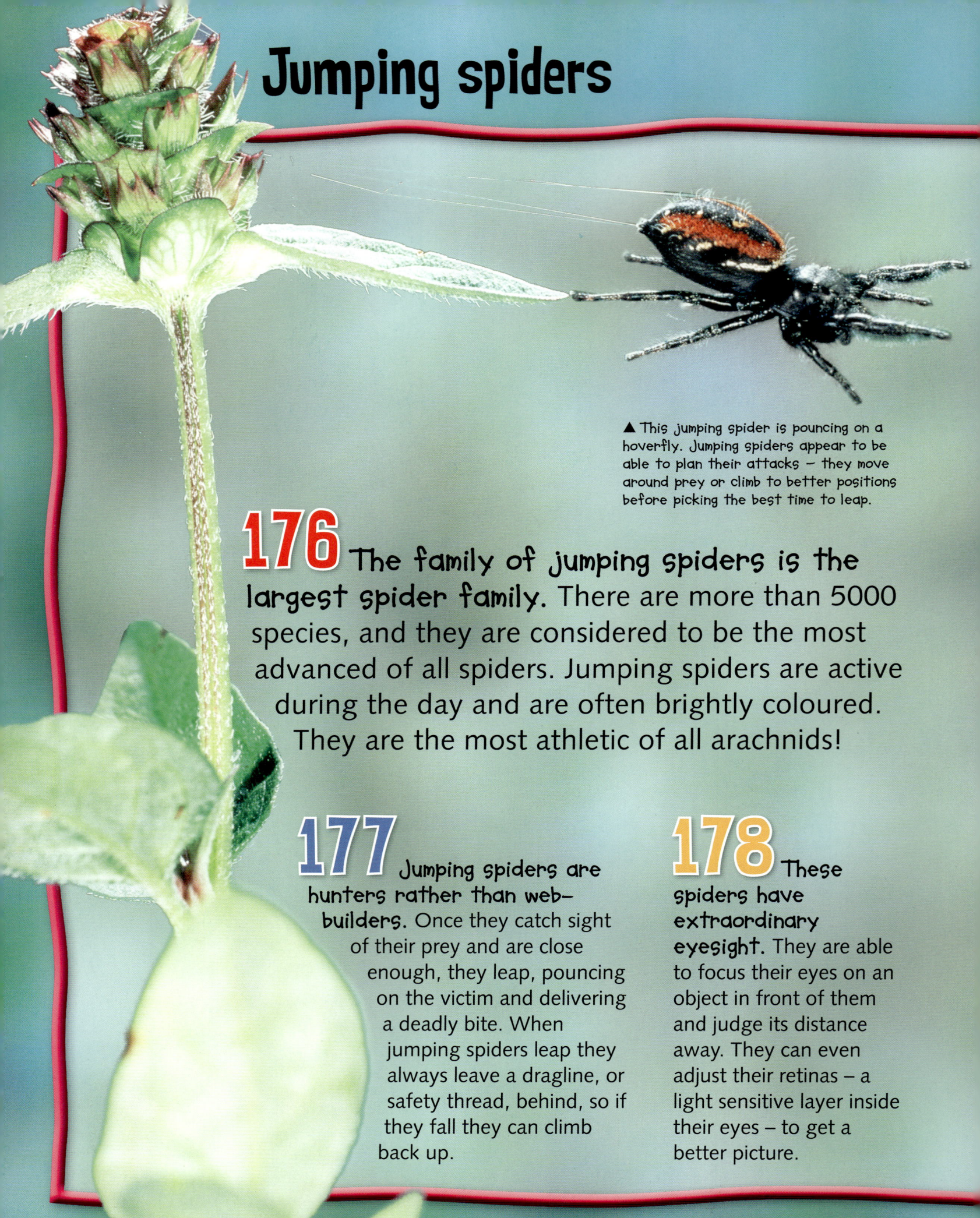

Jumping spiders

▲ This jumping spider is pouncing on a hoverfly. Jumping spiders appear to be able to plan their attacks — they move around prey or climb to better positions before picking the best time to leap.

176 The family of jumping spiders is the largest spider family. There are more than 5000 species, and they are considered to be the most advanced of all spiders. Jumping spiders are active during the day and are often brightly coloured. They are the most athletic of all arachnids!

177 Jumping spiders are hunters rather than web-builders. Once they catch sight of their prey and are close enough, they leap, pouncing on the victim and delivering a deadly bite. When jumping spiders leap they always leave a dragline, or safety thread, behind, so if they fall they can climb back up.

178 These spiders have extraordinary eyesight. They are able to focus their eyes on an object in front of them and judge its distance away. They can even adjust their retinas — a light sensitive layer inside their eyes — to get a better picture.

SPIDERS

QUIZ

If a jumping spider is 10 millimetres long and leaps 20 times its own length, how far will it have travelled? What is that distance in centimetres and in metres?

Answer:
10 × 20 = 200 millimetres
200 millimetres = 20 centimetres or 0.2 metre

179 Scientists think that jumping spiders may be the brainiest of all arachnids. They can use information from their eyes to judge speed, angles and distances, as well as determine if a creature is a predator or prey. Most spiders need to use other sensory information, such as vibrations and smell.

180 Some jumping spiders can leap more than 20 times their own body length. Jumping spiders use their third and fourth pairs of legs to leap, but no one knows what other tricks they might use to achieve their record-breaking long-jumps.

▼ A jumping spider's four main eyes focus on its prey, such as this cricket. The four smaller eyes can detect movement.

Tarantulas

181 **Tarantulas, or bird-eating spiders, mostly live in warm and wet tropical places.** Tarantulas hunt their prey rather than build webs. They usually hunt insects, although larger ones can catch frogs, lizards and even small mammals, such as mice.

182 **King baboon spiders hiss at their attackers.** They are powerful predators and hunt other spiders, chicks, reptiles and frogs. When attacked, king baboon spiders rear up on their back legs to show off their large chelicerae, and make a loud hissing noise by rubbing their hairy legs together.

▶ Like other tarantulas, a king baboon spider relies on its size as much as its venom to overpower its prey.

▼ Tarantulas build burrows under rocks, hide beneath logs or rest in silk-lined tunnels.

I DON'T BELIEVE IT!
Tarantulas are the heaviest of all spiders. A female goliath bird-eating spider weighed 155 grams — more than a newborn kitten!

SPIDERS

183 **Tarantulas don't have good eyesight.** They hunt at night and rely on their touch-sensitive hairs to feel vibrations and movement. A hunting tarantula dashes from its burrow to grab prey, piercing it with large, venomous fangs that are up to 2 centimetres long.

▶ An angry tarantula brushes its abdomen with its legs to fire irritating hairs into the air.

184 **If threatened, a tarantula can flick hairs from its abdomen at an attacker.** The hairs are very irritating to mammals, including humans. Despite this, many people enjoy keeping tarantulas, especially Mexican red-knee tarantulas, as pets.

▼ Hawk wasps prey on tarantulas. Some wasps lay their eggs in a spider's body and others feast on them.

185 **Tarantulas have few natural predators, except certain wasps.** These insects are parasites, which means they live off another animal. The wasp uses her sting to paralyze a spider and lay her eggs inside its body. When the eggs hatch, the larvae feed on the spider's body while it is still alive.

Spiders and us

186 Many people are scared of spiders. This fear has led to spiders appearing in stories and myths. An extreme fear of spiders is called arachnophobia. Someone who likes spiders is called an arachnophile. Very few spiders actually pose any threat to humans.

▲ Tarantulas are not ideal pets. They bite, their hairs can be harmful and being handled may cause them stress.

▼ Cooking spiders makes their venom harmless. They are sold as a popular street snack in Cambodia.

187 European tarantulas gave rise to a wild dance called 'the tarantella'. These spiders belong to a different family to the bird-eating tarantulas. They were named after the Italian town of Taranto, where it was believed that the effects of a spider bite could only be relieved by performing a frenzied dance – the tarantella.

188 Some people like eating spiders. In Cambodia, Southeast Asia, spider catchers use sticks to entice tarantulas from their burrows. They are caught, fried, and served with garlic and salt.

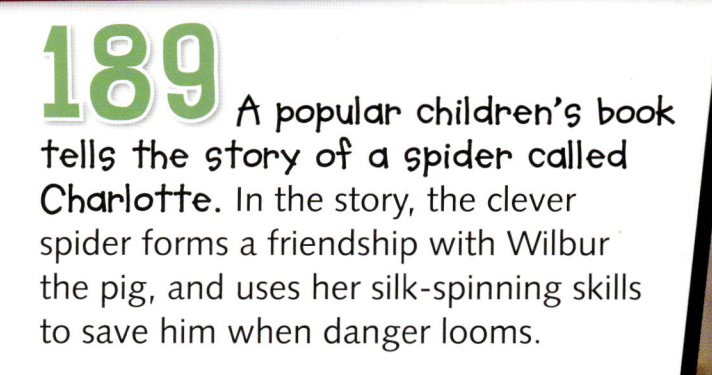

189 A popular children's book tells the story of a spider called Charlotte. In the story, the clever spider forms a friendship with Wilbur the pig, and uses her silk-spinning skills to save him when danger looms.

190 Spider powers were the inspiration for one of the greatest comic book heroes of all time. In the story of Spider-Man, Peter Parker fights crime with the help of web-shooters, spider sense, great strength, and the ability to climb walls and cling to ceilings.

▲ E B White wrote *Charlotte's Web* more than 50 years ago, but it is still a much-loved tale.

▼ The Spider-Man stories have been turned into successful cartoons and action movies. This is a scene from *Spider-Man 2* (2004).

SOS – save our spiders

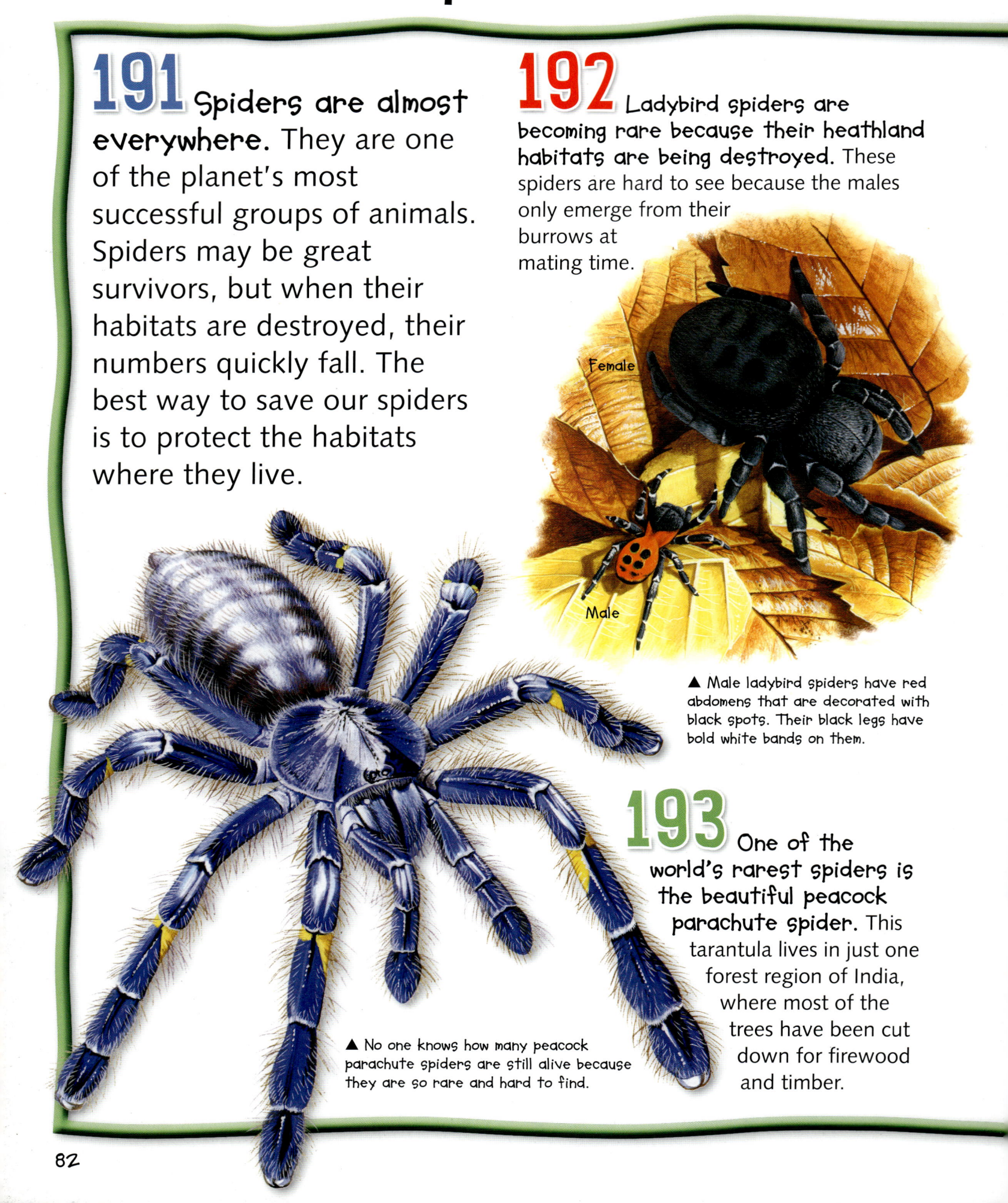

191 Spiders are almost everywhere. They are one of the planet's most successful groups of animals. Spiders may be great survivors, but when their habitats are destroyed, their numbers quickly fall. The best way to save our spiders is to protect the habitats where they live.

192 Ladybird spiders are becoming rare because their heathland habitats are being destroyed. These spiders are hard to see because the males only emerge from their burrows at mating time.

Female
Male

▲ Male ladybird spiders have red abdomens that are decorated with black spots. Their black legs have bold white bands on them.

193 One of the world's rarest spiders is the beautiful peacock parachute spider. This tarantula lives in just one forest region of India, where most of the trees have been cut down for firewood and timber.

▲ No one knows how many peacock parachute spiders are still alive because they are so rare and hard to find.

SPIDERS

I DON'T BELIEVE IT!
Scientists predict that nearly 30 species of spider could become extinct in the near future.

194 No-eyed big-eyed wolf spiders live in just three volcanic caves on the Hawaiian island of Kaua'i. These arachnids have lost their eyes after living in dark caves for thousands of years or more. There are only about 100 adult no-eyed big-eyed wolf spiders left. They need their habitats to be damp, but pollution and farming have affected them, causing the caves to become too dry.

195 Spiders are an essential part of Earth's web of life. They provide food for many animals and feed on other creatures. Spiders help to maintain the balance of life on our planet, which would be a terrible place without them. A spider in the bath should be admired, not washed away!

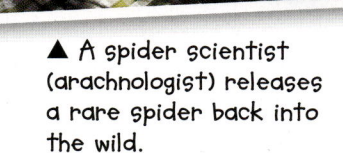

▲ A spider scientist (arachnologist) releases a rare spider back into the wild.

▶ A curious house spider eyes a plughole. Once you understand how spiders live, they become fascinating, not frightening, creatures.

BUTTERFLIES & MOTHS

196 In the natural world, at almost any moment, a winged creature might silently flutter by. This is a glimpse of the fascinating insect group called butterflies and moths. There are thousands of different kinds, and they range in size from smaller than this 'o', to bigger than this page. They are vital to the places in which they live (habitats) – yet many are under threat from human activity.

◀ The name of the silver-washed fritillary butterfly comes from the silvery sheen under its wings.

▶ Many moths are dull grey or brown in colour, but the crimson speckled moth has vivid markings.

Scale wings

197 Butterflies and moths belong to the insect group Lepidoptera. It contains more than 180,000 different kinds, or species. This is more than almost any other animal group, except beetles and flies. Moth species outnumber butterflies by about 10 to 1. Their closest insect cousins are caddisflies.

BUTTERFLIES
- Hesperiidae — Skippers
- Papilionoidea — 'Typical' butterflies
- Hedylidae — Moth-butterflies
- Papilionidae — Swallowtails, birdwings and others
- Pieridae — Whites, yellows and oranges
- Lycaenidae — Blues, coppers and hairstreaks
- Riodinidae — Metalmarks
- Nymphalidae — Brush-footed butterflies such as emperors, monarchs and fritillaries

198 Like most insects, butterflies and moths have a three-part body. At the front is the head with the mouthparts, eyes and antennae. In the middle is the thorax, with six legs and four wings. At the rear is a long abdomen. Yet butterflies and moths differ from other insects in their wings and mouthparts.

KEY
1. Wings
2. Thorax
3. Abdomen
4. Head
5. Eyes
6. Antennae
7. Legs

▶ A lepidopteran's wings and legs are all attached to its thorax.

BUTTERFLIES & MOTHS

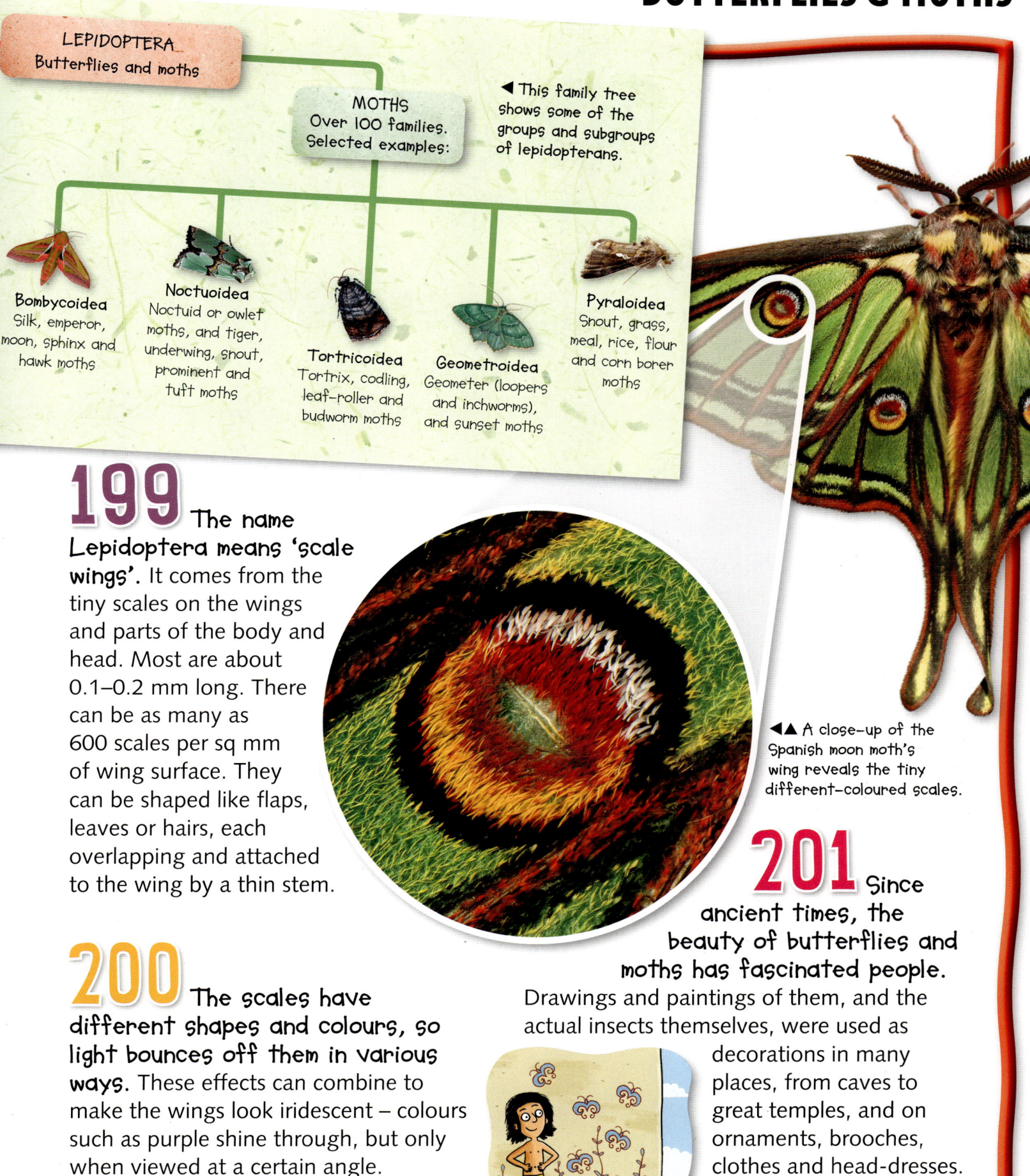

LEPIDOPTERA
Butterflies and moths

MOTHS
Over 100 families.
Selected examples:

◄ This family tree shows some of the groups and subgroups of lepidopterans.

Bombycoidea
Silk, emperor, moon, sphinx and hawk moths

Noctuoidea
Noctuid or owlet moths, and tiger, underwing, snout, prominent and tuft moths

Tortricoidea
Tortrix, codling, leaf-roller and budworm moths

Geometroidea
Geometer (loopers and inchworms), and sunset moths

Pyraloidea
Snout, grass, meal, rice, flour and corn borer moths

199 The name Lepidoptera means 'scale wings'. It comes from the tiny scales on the wings and parts of the body and head. Most are about 0.1–0.2 mm long. There can be as many as 600 scales per sq mm of wing surface. They can be shaped like flaps, leaves or hairs, each overlapping and attached to the wing by a thin stem.

◄◄▲ A close-up of the Spanish moon moth's wing reveals the tiny different-coloured scales.

200 The scales have different shapes and colours, so light bounces off them in various ways. These effects can combine to make the wings look iridescent – colours such as purple shine through, but only when viewed at a certain angle.

201 Since ancient times, the beauty of butterflies and moths has fascinated people. Drawings and paintings of them, and the actual insects themselves, were used as decorations in many places, from caves to great temples, and on ornaments, brooches, clothes and head-dresses.

Moth or butterfly?

Love the light
In the hot African sun, small striped swordtail butterflies flock to sip mineral-rich water at the edge of a drying waterhole.

Fly-by-night
The gold swift moth of Europe is beautifully camouflaged to hide among old leaves, twigs and stems by day. It then emerges at dusk.

Day-flier
The Asian butterfly hawk moth is strong and fast. It flies speedily by day, searching for food and mates.

▲ Most moths are night-active, but not all.

202 There are several main differences between butterflies and moths. However, there are exceptions to all of them. For example, most butterflies are active by day, or diurnal, while moths tend to fly at night – nocturnal. Yet some moths, like the butterfly hawk moth, are day-fliers.

203 Butterflies generally have colourful wings and slender bodies. Many moths are brown, grey or similar dull colours, and have stout bodies. But there are many brilliantly colourful moths, especially in warm parts of the world.

▼ When resting, most moths hold their wings out flat, while butterflies fold them together over the back.

Bright and slender
The thin-bodied malachite butterfly, found in parts of the Americas, is named after the green mineral malachite.

Furry emperor
The Ligurnian emperor moth of central Europe has a hairy thorax and abdomen, and false 'eyes' on its wings.

Colourful creature
The day-flying false tiger moth of southern and southeast Asia has brilliant colours to warn predators it has a foul taste.

KEY
- 🟠 Butterflies
- 🟢 Moths
- 🩷 Exceptions

Alert antennae
In northwest North America, Taylor's checkerspot butterfly uses its wide-ended antennae to detect flower scents.

Feathery feelers
The male Japanese luna moth spreads his plume-like antennae to catch the pheromones (special scents) released by females of his species.

204 Most butterflies have slim antennae with a wider part at the end, known as club-ended. Many moths have antennae that taper to a point, and in the males are frilly or feathery. But the castiniid moth family have club-ended antennae.

Club-ended
Australia's golden sun moth, one of the few species with clubbed antennae, is critically endangered in its specialized grassland habitat.

◀▲ All butterflies have club-ended antennae; very few moths do.

205 When a butterfly caterpillar enters the next stage of its life, it changes into a hard-cased pupa, or chrysalis. Many moth caterpillars also make an extra covering of silky threads, called a cocoon. Unusually, apollo butterflies spin cocoons like moths.

Soft touch
The ruby tiger moth of Europe and north Asia wraps itself in a cocoon of strong threads as it develops, or metamorphoses, into an adult.

▼▶ Only a few butterfly caterpillars spin cocoons.

206 Most moths have a tiny rod or spine, called a frenulum, near the body at the front of each rear wing. This fits into a hook known as the retinaculum, at the base of the front wing. This pairing makes the two wings on each side move together more effectively. Very few butterflies have this feature.

Hard cases
Found in southeast Asia, pupae of the large tree nymph butterfly are well-known for their shiny golden cases.

Silken cocoon
The clouded apollo butterfly of north Asia and Europe spins a cocoon of silken threads on the ground.

A closer look

207 Like other insects, butterflies and moths have a hard outer body covering called an exoskeleton. This is made of a tough substance called chitin. The exoskeleton covers nearly all of the body, even the legs and antennae, and gives strength and protection to the soft parts inside.

▼ This cutaway diagram shows the inner parts of the female golden birdwing butterfly.

THORAX

208 The head has the mouthparts for feeding, including a long tube called the proboscis. Also on the head are the main sense organs such as the eyes and antennae (see page 92). Inside is the tiny brain, as small as the dot on this 'i'.

KEY		
1 Head	8 Lateral trachea	15 Main blood vessel
2 Eye	9 Main dorsal trachea	16 Hearts
3 Brain	10 Fore (front) wing	17 Main nerve
4 Oesophagus	11 Hind (rear) wing	18 Crop (stomach)
5 Antenna	12 Fore (front) leg	19 Gut (intestines)
6 Proboscis	13 Middle leg	20 Excretory system
7 Spiracles	14 Hind (rear) leg	21 Reproductive parts

QUIZ

Where are these parts on a butterfly or moth?
1. Waste removal system
2. Eyes
3. Wing-moving muscles
4. Veins

Answers:
1. Abdomen 2. Head 3. Thorax 4. Wings

BUTTERFLIES & MOTHS

209 Behind the head, the thorax is like a stiff, strong box. The wings and legs are attached to it by flexible joints. Inside it are powerful muscles that move the wings and legs. Through it passes the feeding tube, or oesophagus.

210 The fore or front wings, and the hind or rear wings, are wide, flat and thin. They are strengthened by tube-like structures called veins, which contain air tubes and a blood-like fluid, haemolymph. The fore wings are usually larger and more pointed, making them move through the air more easily.

▶ The wing veins of this common emigrant butterfly have a branching pattern.

211 Like other insects, butterflies and moths have three pairs of legs. Each is covered in scales and has about nine tube-like sections, ending in a foot with tiny claws or brush-like hairs.

▶ This geometer moth foot has tiny scales, two gripping claws and touch-sensitive hairs.

212 The abdomen contains the main digestive parts (crop and intestines), the excretory (waste-removal) system, and the reproductive parts. Like most of the body it has small air holes called spiracles. These lead to a network of tubes called the trachea that are the breathing system, passing air to all body parts.

Super senses

There are long, thin muscles inside the antenna, allowing it to bend

213 Butterflies and moths have two antenna, or feelers. Their tiny sensors detect substances they touch and also those in the air – such as pheromones released at breeding time. Antennae also respond to heat, cold, and moving air or wind.

▼ Each eye has thousands of individual parts, forming a dome shape. This allows the butterfly or moth to detect movement over a wide area.

214 A butterfly or moth eye is compound, made up of many tiny lenses called ommatidia. Each detects a small area of the insect's view, and these many areas are combined by the brain into one large image, like a mosaic. The eyes can see certain colours and also ultraviolet light (which human eyes cannot detect). Some flowers have patterns that only show up in ultraviolet light, guiding the moth or butterfly to the nectar that it feeds on.

▶ Invisible in normal light (left), the marsh marigold's nectar guide patterns show up in ultraviolet light (right).

In normal light

Nerve to brain
Light-sensitive cells
Pigment (coloured) cells
Rhabdom (central rod)
Crystalline cone of lens
Cornea of lens

◀ Each ommatidium lets in light through a lens at the wide end.

BUTTERFLIES & MOTHS

215 Butterflies and moths can 'hear' with their antennae. They can also 'hear' with thin, bendy patches on the body surface that vibrate when hit by sound waves. These are called tympanal organs, and are usually on the thorax.

217 Tiger moths have thorax patches called tymbals that vibrate to send out sounds. These confuse bats trying to use the echoes of their own high-pitched sounds to navigate and hunt in the dark.

216 Some moths have 'ears' or tympanal organs on different parts of their bodies. Geometer moths have theirs at the front of the abdomen. Noctuid moths have them on the wings, to sense the clicks and squeaks of bats who hunt them at night.

218 Tiny organs allow butterflies and moths to both 'smell' and 'taste' with their feet. Known as olfactory organs, they respond to certain substances floating in the air (smell) and on surfaces (taste). So a butterfly or moth can tell as soon as it lands if a place is likely to have food or be harmful.

▶ Olfactory or smell organs are on various parts of this Chinese peacock butterfly, including its antennae and feet.

In ultraviolet light

Food and feeding

219 Most adult butterflies and moths have a long, tube-like mouthpart, the proboscis. Hardly any other insect has this. The proboscis is usually coiled up in a spiral under the head. To feed, it unrolls and works like a straw to suck up liquid foods or small food particles.

220 Some types of moth have a strong enough proboscis to pierce the skin of fresh citrus fruits. They do this to feed on the juice inside. These moths are thought of as pests by farmers.

221 The main food of butterflies and moths is nectar, a sugary liquid that comes from flowers. They find nectar using their antennae, eyes, and smell and taste sensors on their feet. Another food is pollen grains, tiny particles made by male flower parts, which join with female parts to develop seeds and fruits.

Coiled up proboscis

▲ The coiled proboscis tucks out of the way under the head.

◀ The uncoiled proboscis can be longer than the whole body, as in Morgan's sphinx moth.

222 Insects that carry pollen are vital for flowers to reproduce. Butterflies and moths are second only to bees and wasps in helping this process. Certain flowers open only at the time of day or night, or year, when the butterflies and moths that feed on them are on the wing (active).

▲ Buddleia is known as the 'butterfly bush', as its nectar-rich flowers attract many species, such as these small tortoiseshell butterflies.

▼ A black king butterfly straightens its proboscis to sip from a puddle.

▼ Some pools attract large numbers of butterflies, like these orange sulphurs.

223 Some butterflies and moths feed on more unusual liquids. These include rotting fruit juices, and animal sweat, tears, urine or dung. Others gather at waterholes or muddy pools and 'puddle' – suck up the water to obtain nutrients. However, some have no working mouthparts and so do not feed at all.

224 Adult butterflies and moths rarely cause problems with their feeding. But a few species of caterpillars can be huge pests to people, causing damage worth millions of pounds. Different kinds eat farm crops, fruits, vegetables, garden flowers, tree buds and blossom, stored grains and other foods – even our clothes. The clothes moth caterpillar feeds on fabrics made of wool and other natural fibres.

Getting together

225 To breed or reproduce – make more of their kind – a female and male of the same species get together to mate. In many butterflies, the female and male look different – this is called sexual dimorphism. For example, the male adonis blue is bright blue in colour, while the female is dull blue-grey. The male vapourer moth has red-brown wings, but the female has tiny wings and cannot even fly.

▼ The male (below) and female (left) adonis blue butterflies almost look like different species.

226 In many moths, the female gives off special scents called pheromones from her abdomen. A male of her kind can detect it with his wide feathery antennae, perhaps from a kilometre or more away. The male of one of the largest moths, the atlas moth, has extra-large feathery antennae. Some males also make pheromones.

QUIZ

1. What colour is the female adonis blue butterfly?
2. What is the name of the special scents given off by females?
3. Why do males and females make courtship movements?

Answers:
1. Dull blue-grey 2. Pheromones 3. To check that the other is a suitable partner

BUTTERFLIES & MOTHS

227 **Usually the male butterfly or moth actively seeks out the female.** Day-flying species often do this by sight. The male Australian painted lady butterfly perches on a tall tree or hilltop, to watch for females flying past. Male purple emperors occupy a certain area, called their territory, and fight off other males who try to enter.

▲ Male purple emperors flap in battle, one showing eye-like underwing spots.

228 **As they meet, the male and female make certain movements known as courtship.** This is to check that the other is healthy and a suitable partner. For example, paper kite butterflies flutter and dance around each other slowly and gracefully in a courtship flight, like kites swooping in the wind.

229 **Adult butterflies are usually short-lived and so must breed quickly.** For example, the spring azure and small blue live as adults for only a few days. A few species survive as adults for a year or slightly more, such as the mourning cloak (Camberwell beauty), brimstone and red postman.

▶ Due to their fluttering courtship dance, these butterflies are known by names such as paper kite, rice paper or handkerchief butterflies.

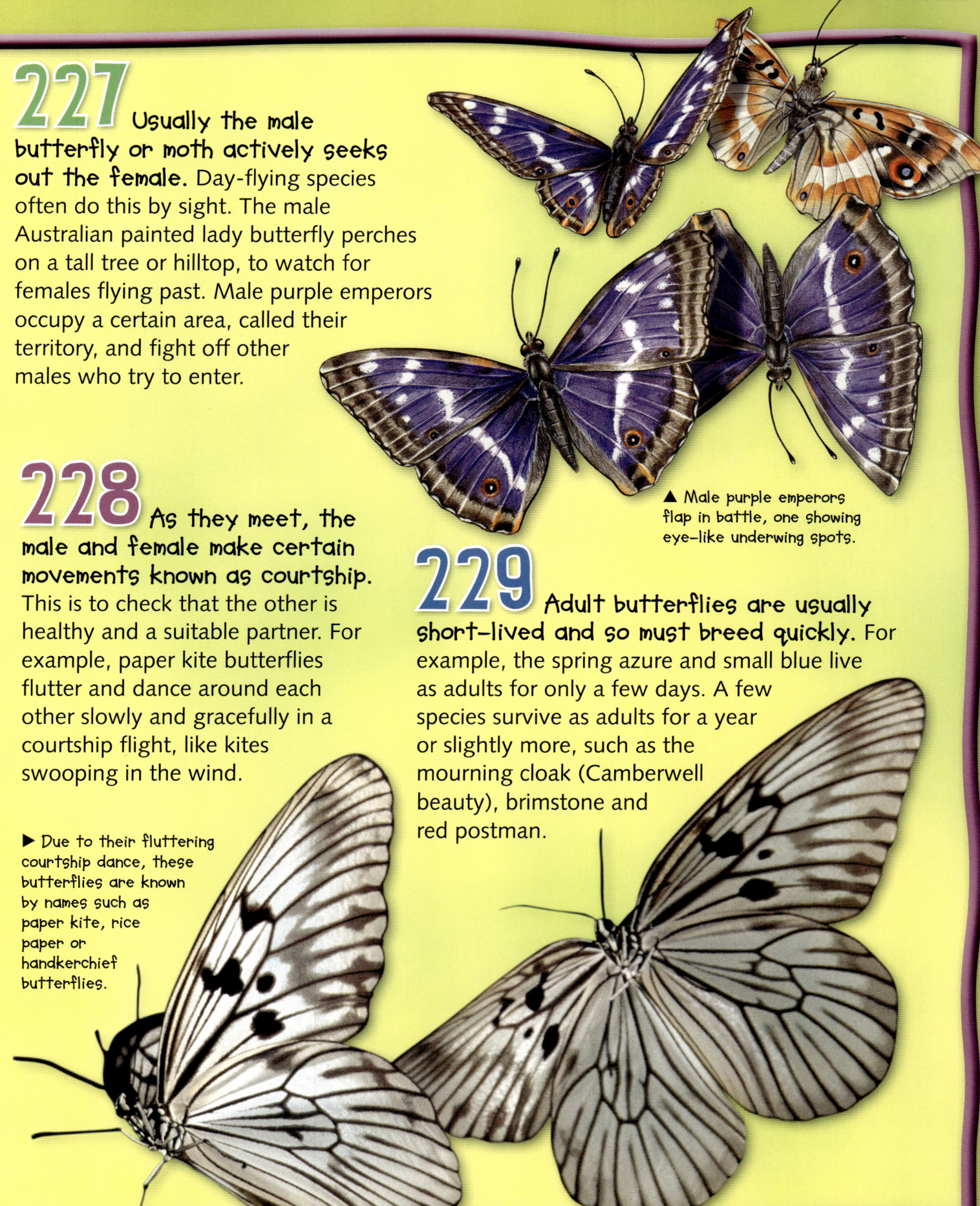

97

Growing up

230 Butterflies and moths grow up in a series of stages, known as the life cycle. During these stages – egg, caterpillar, chrysalis and adult – they change their shape greatly. This process is called metamorphosis. The adult female usually lays eggs on or near the plants the caterpillars will eat when they hatch. Ghost moths may lay over 10,000 eggs in one go.

231 The eggs hatch into caterpillars, or larvae. They start to eat at once. Few other animals have such huge appetites for their size. Most species have particular food plants, for example, small tortoiseshell, red admiral and peacock butterfly caterpillars all eat stinging nettles.

232 The caterpillar's exoskeleton cannot stretch much. So after a time it splits, the caterpillar wiggles out, enlarges and forms a new, bigger casing. This is known as shedding, moulting or ecdysis. Most caterpillars do this five times. Each stage is called an instar.

1. The female swallowtail butterfly lays its eggs on milk parsley, wild carrot, wild angelica, fennel, hogweed or clover. Only one egg is laid at a time

2. This first instar (stage) caterpillar is three days old and as small as a rice grain

▶ Selected stages from the life cycle of the Old World or common swallowtail butterfly.

3. By the third instar the caterpillar (larva) has grown hundreds of times bigger

BUTTERFLIES & MOTHS

The adult Old World swallowtail is a powerful flier

The adult swallowtail rests after emerging from its chrysalis casing

The chrysalis is well camouflaged as an old leaf or twig. It is held upright on the twig by a silk loop

The fifth instar caterpillar prepares to form a hard case around itself and become a chrysalis (pupa)

233 At its last moult, the caterpillar develops a tougher, different-shaped casing and becomes a chrysalis, or pupa. In many moth species the caterpillar spins a cocoon of silk threads around itself as an extra covering. The pupa looks inactive, but inside, its body parts are changing.

234 Eventually the pupa splits open, and out squeezes the adult, or imago. Once its crumpled wings and other parts have enlarged and hardened, it is ready to fly, feed and breed.

235 The length of the life cycle varies according to the species, temperature and food supply. It can take from a month to a year, and in some cases even longer. Some species spend a harsh time of year, such as winter or drought, as caterpillars, while others spend it as pupae, adults or eggs.

I DON'T BELIEVE IT!
In many species, the new caterpillar's first meal is its egg case, which contains lots of nutrients. Likewise, older caterpillars often eat their cast-off casings.

Clever caterpillars

236 Caterpillars look very different from adult butterflies and moths. They lack wings, and the head, thorax and abdomen are difficult to tell apart. They have small eyes and feelers shaped like teeth, called palps, to taste food. Instead of a proboscis, caterpillars have scissor-like mouthparts called mandibles, to cut and chew food.

▶ A caterpillar's 'jaws' or mandibles work with a side-to-side motion, like hook-shaped scissors.

Mandible   Palp

237 A caterpillar has three pairs of legs on the thorax, like an adult, although these are much shorter. It also has up to five extra pairs of stumpy legs on the abdomen, known as prolegs. The caterpillar crawls by moving these legs forwards and backwards, and also makes its body longer and shorter by arching up and down.

◀ 'Looper' caterpillars arch the front of the body up, extend forwards and down, then pull the rear along too.

238 Caterpillars are vital parts of nature's food chains. They are soft and slow, and so can be easy prey for predators such as shrews, rats, birds, lizards, frogs and praying mantises. Millions of caterpillars are eaten every year.

Prolegs

BUTTERFLIES & MOTHS

239 However, many caterpillars can defend themselves. Some taste horrible, due to substances they get from their food. They often have bright markings in 'warning colours' such as red, yellow and black. Predators will remember the bad taste and avoid similar colours in future.

240 Some caterpillars have a coat of long hairs to protect themselves. These break easily to release a fluid that stings or irritates the predator. Such caterpillars are often known as 'woolly bears'.

241 Hawaiian eupithecia moth caterpillars are sneaky hunters. They pretend to be twigs, then pounce on creatures such as snails, flies and even small frogs.

▶ The garden tiger moth's 'woolly bear' caterpillar has long hairs, setae, that cause redness and irritation when touched.

242 Another method of defence is for a caterpillar to rear up and look fierce. In doing this, some display bright eye-like patterns, wave a long 'horn' or squirt foul liquid. The puss moth caterpillar has a bendy red section on each of its tails that flick to frighten predators.

◀ The puss moth caterpillar displays its red front and flips its long tail whips at enemies.

Families of moths

243 Animals that are closely related and similar to each other are organized into groups called families. There are more than 100 main families of moths. Some consist of thousands of species, others far fewer. The Opostegidae family, known as white eyecap moths, has fewer than 200 species.

Geometrid family

▲ This geometrid 'looper' caterpillar is coloured to resemble a small twig.

244 **The largest moth family is the noctuids or owlet moths.** It has more than 35,000 species – about one in five of all moths. The owlet, underwing, dagger, forester, dart and silver-Y moths all belong to this group. Most are dull-coloured, but the burnished brass moth has bright metallic patches on its upper wings.

▶ The burnished brass moth has shiny green patches like old brass.

ACTUAL SIZE

Noctuid family

245 Another very large family is the geometrids or geometer moths, with about 26,000 species. It includes wave, mocha and emerald moths. Their caterpillars are known as loopers, spanworms or inchworms from the way they arch their bodies into an upside-down U or loop as they move along.

BUTTERFLIES & MOTHS

246 The saturnid family includes royal, emperor, atlas and giant moths, with around 2000 species. They are among the biggest of all moths, and of all lepidopterans – even of all insects. The regal moth of North America has greyish wings 15 centimetres across, with brown stripes and pale spots.

247 At night some moths fly towards lights. They are thought to use the moon to fly straight, keeping it at the same angle to their path, but they are confused by artificial lights as the angle changes when they fly past.

Saturnid family

▶ The adult regal moth has no working mouthparts and only lives for about a week.

ACTUAL SIZE

Sphingid family

248 Hawk moths and sphinx moths belong to the sphingid family. It has about 1500 species. Sphingids have large bodies and sweptback wings that beat very rapidly, making them speedy fliers. Some hawk moths can even hover in mid-air, like flies and hummingbirds.

◀ The bee hawk moth hovers near a flower, preparing to feed.

103

Butterfly families

249 Like moths, closely related butterflies are grouped into families. The largest is the nymphalids, with over 6000 species such as emperors, monarchs, admirals and fritillaries. In most, the front legs are unusually small with brush-like ends, giving them the name brush-footed butterflies. The upper wing surfaces are brightly coloured.

Nymphalid family

▲ The great purple emperor, a nymphalid, is patterned above but its underwings are plain.

250 The lycaenid family is the second biggest. It has more than 5000 species of blues, coppers, hairstreaks, elfins, harvesters and woolly-legs. They are generally small and shiny. In certain species their caterpillars feed on insects such as aphids and ants.

251 The hesperiids, or skippers, are named after their fast darting or 'skipping' flight. Skippers are often classified separately from butterflies. They have moth-like features such as a tubby body and relatively small wings, and antennae with hooked or bent ends, rather than clubbed.

▼ A slug-like lycaenid moth-butterfly caterpillar preys on ant larvae.

Lycaenid family

252 Swallowtails, birdwings and apollos are in the papilionid family. Most of the 550 species are big and brightly coloured, with trailing flaps, tails or strips on the rear wings that resemble the deep-forked tail of the swallow bird.

▼ A common rose swallowtail shows its streamer-like rear wing 'tails'.

Papilionid family

▼ Hedylids are classed as butterflies but have many moth-like features, such as drab colours.

Hedylid family

253 The pierid family contains some 1100 species of whites, yellows, sulphurs, orange-tips and oranges. Some have dark spots and patches. Another small family, with 1500 species, is the shiny-winged riodinids. They include harlequin and punch butterflies. The smallest is the moth-like hedylids or American moth-butterflies, with 35 species.

▼ Riodinids such as the common red harlequin are known as metalmarks due to their shiny patches.

ACTUAL SIZE

Riodinid family

MAKE A NEW SPECIES

You will need:
thin card scissors glue shiny coloured paper, foil, sweet wrappers, etc.

Draw and cut out a big butterfly shape using the card. Cut out shiny coloured circles, diamonds, stripes and other shapes and glue them onto the wings. Think of a name for your new species, make a label and put it on display.

Cunning camouflage

254 Few creatures have such amazing camouflage as adult butterflies and moths. They often look like common objects found in nature that are not tasty or edible, so predators leave them alone. Hunters of butterflies and moths include many birds that can see well in colour, which is why camouflage is so important.

255 The false burnet moth spins an unusual gold-coloured cocoon. Hanging from a branch, it resembles a small version of the net or bag we buy oranges in.

256 Many moths are inactive by day and are camouflaged as twigs, dead leaves, bark and stones. Peppered moths exactly match the lichen-covered tree trunks where they rest. Some butterflies close their wings to hide the bright upper surfaces. The lower surfaces can look like leaves, either fresh and green, or brown and dead.

LIGHT AND DARK
Most peppered moths have pale and dark speckles (right) for camouflage on lichen-covered trees. Darker or melanic forms (left) regularly occur but they are easily seen and caught by predators.

During the Industrial Revolution, trees became covered in soot. The melanic form was better camouflaged and so became more common. Less pollution in modern times means the original form is again becoming more common.

▶ The Kallima dead-leaf butterfly bears an astonishing resemblance to an old brown leaf, even down to the veins.

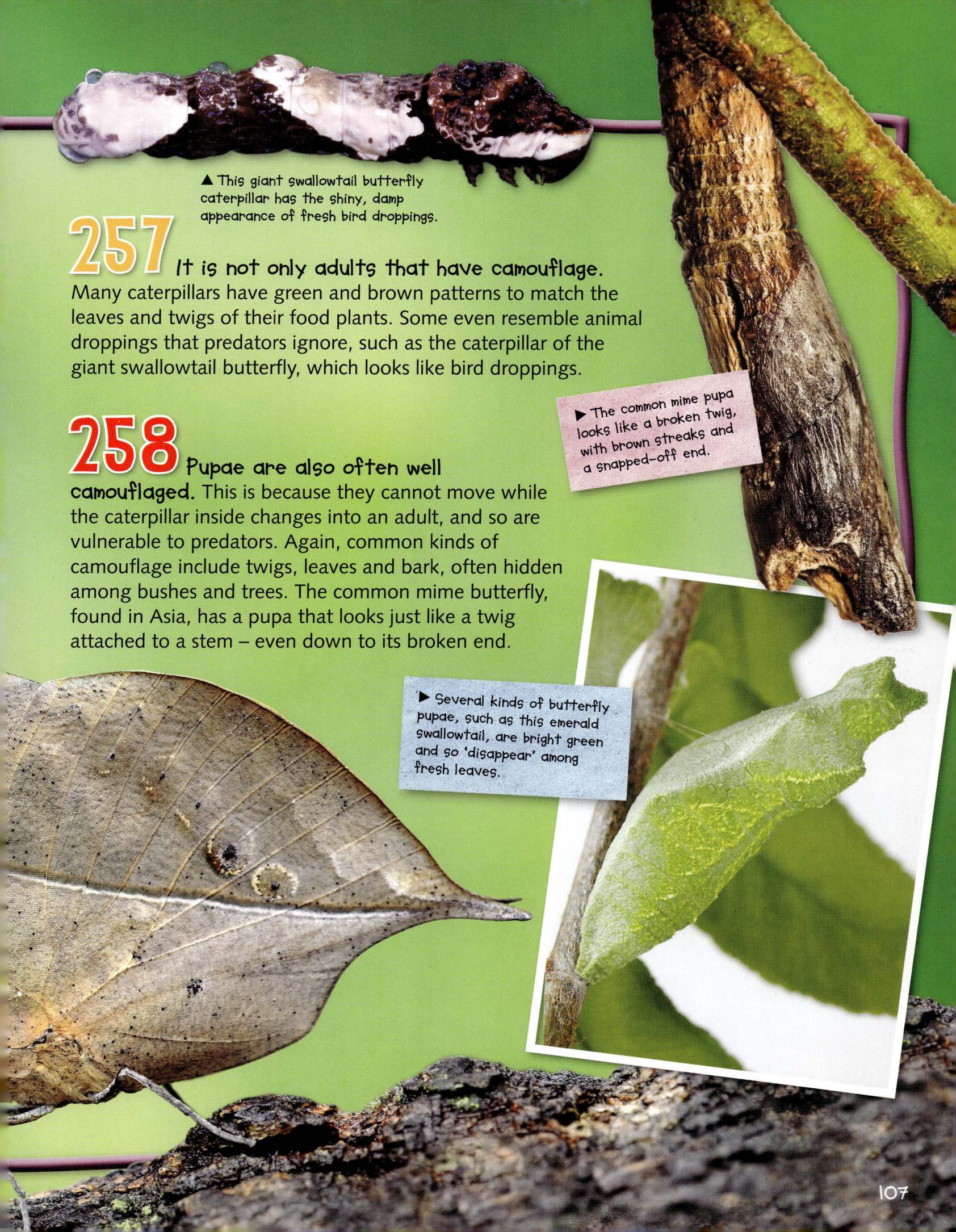

▲ This giant swallowtail butterfly caterpillar has the shiny, damp appearance of fresh bird droppings.

257 **It is not only adults that have camouflage.** Many caterpillars have green and brown patterns to match the leaves and twigs of their food plants. Some even resemble animal droppings that predators ignore, such as the caterpillar of the giant swallowtail butterfly, which looks like bird droppings.

258 **Pupae are also often well camouflaged.** This is because they cannot move while the caterpillar inside changes into an adult, and so are vulnerable to predators. Again, common kinds of camouflage include twigs, leaves and bark, often hidden among bushes and trees. The common mime butterfly, found in Asia, has a pupa that looks just like a twig attached to a stem – even down to its broken end.

▶ The common mime pupa looks like a broken twig, with brown streaks and a snapped-off end.

▶ Several kinds of butterfly pupae, such as this emerald swallowtail, are bright green and so 'disappear' among fresh leaves.

107

Survival tricks

259 Butterflies and moths use trickery, deceit and pretence to survive. Some have large rounded eye-like patterns, eyespots, on their wings. These are usually hidden, but the butterfly or moth can suddenly move its wings to display them. They look like the eyes of a cat, hawk, owl or similar fierce creature, and so can frighten away predators.

▲ The Io moth's front wings move aside to reveal glaring predator-like 'eyes' on its rear wings.

260 Like caterpillars, some adults have bright warning colours and patterns, such as yellow and black, or red and black. These tell predators that they taste horrible or are poisonous. After a predator has tried to eat one, it recognizes the warning colours and avoids others with those colours.

261 Different distasteful species sometimes have very similar warning colours. After a predator encounters one of them, it avoids any similar-coloured creatures. This kind of similarity is known as Mullerian mimicry.

▼ Tiger-striped, tiger and numata longwing butterflies share similar colours to show they taste horrible.

Tiger-striped longwing

Tiger longwing

Numata longwing

◀ The pipevine swallowtail's flesh tastes foul, yet its mimic...

◀ ...the spicebush swallowtail, which looks so similar, is tasty to predators.

262 Other species have warning colours – yet they are quite tasty! This kind of pretence is called Batesian mimicry. The pretender, or mimic, looks similar to a distasteful or poisonous species, so predators tend to avoid the mimic as well.

263 In other forms of mimicry, butterflies and moths pretend to be very different kinds of animals. They mimic creatures that their predators do not usually eat, such as wasps and spiders, and even toads and snakes. The atlas moth's front wingtip resembles a snake's head, complete with eye and mouth slit.

ACTUAL SIZE

◀ The Atlas moth's snake-head wing pattern.

264 There can also be different colour forms of the same species. Known as polymorphs, these breed together as usual, but they look quite unlike each other. Each form, or morph, may mimic another, different species. So for a predator, knowing which species is which, and whether it tastes good or bad, is difficult.

QUIZ

1. Which colours are examples of warning colours?
2. Which animal does the atlas moth's front wingtip resemble?
3. What is the name for different colour forms of the same species?

Answers:
1. Yellow and black, and red and black 2. A snake 3. Polymorphs

On the wing

265 Nearly all kinds of butterflies and moths can fly as adults. They fly to avoid predators, find food, locate mates, and in some species, travel to places with better conditions. Despite their delicate appearance, they are powerful fliers. However, some female moths have tiny wings or none at all, such as the winter moth.

266 Butterfly and moth wings beat in a similar way to those of some other insects. They are hinged onto the thorax, which is like a stiff box. Two sets of muscles inside the thorax make it alternately lower, then higher, causing the wings to flick up and down.

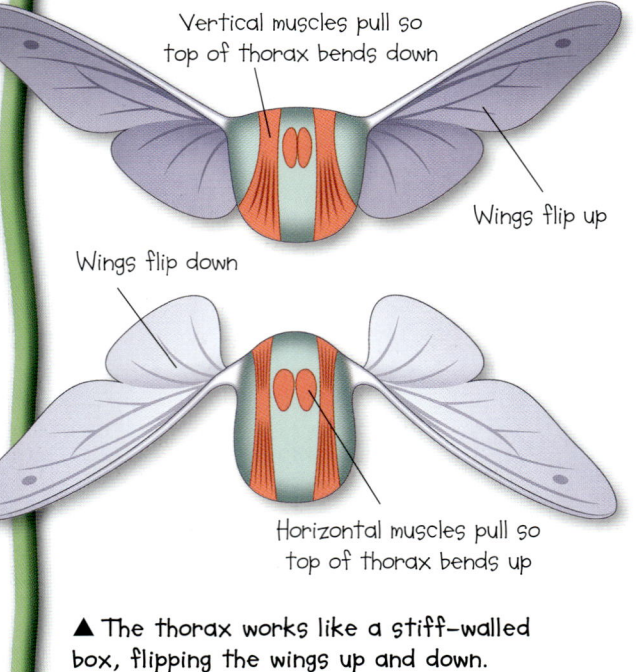

QUIZ

1. Are male or female winter moths flightless?
2. Where are the muscles that allow the wings to flap?
3. Where do bogong moths migrate from?

Answers:
1. Female 2. In the thorax 3. The plains of New South Wales and Queensland in Australia

- Vertical muscles pull so top of thorax bends down
- Wings flip up
- Wings flip down
- Horizontal muscles pull so top of thorax bends up

▲ The thorax works like a stiff-walled box, flipping the wings up and down.

▼ In general, larger species of butterflies and moths flap their wings more slowly than smaller ones.

How fast do they flap?

Atlas moths
Number of wingbeats per second: **5–10**

White butterflies
Number of wingbeats per second: **12**

Skipper butterflies
Number of wingbeats per second: **20**

Cutworm moths
Number of wingbeats per second: **30–60**

Leaf-miner moths
Number of wingbeats per second: **over 200**

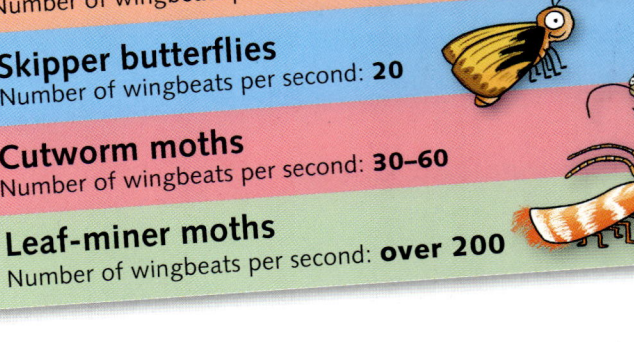

267 Although most remain in a small area, some species take to the air in mass flights for long-distance migrations. The monarch butterfly is famous for this (see next page). Every year in Australia, millions of bogong moths migrate from the plains of New South Wales and Queensland, to spend summer in the cooler Snowy Mountains to the south. Attracted by the lights, they land in huge numbers in cities such as Canberra and Sydney.

▲ Migrating bogong moths can cause chaos in cities, getting into buildings and vehicles and clogging up air conditioning.

▲ The two wings on either side change angle as they flap together, as on this cecropia moth.

268 Certain butterflies and moths undergo irruptions. This is when good conditions every few years, such as calm weather and plenty of food, mean there's a huge increase in numbers. They then fly off in swarms to find new places to feed and breed. This happens occasionally to underwing moths in parts of Europe.

The greatest traveller

269 Of all butterflies and moths, the North American monarch or milkweed butterfly is the greatest traveller. In winter, adults roost (rest) on trees in California, Florida and other southern states, as well as Mexico – all places with mild winters. At some roosts, many thousands of adults cluster together.

◀ Trees at monarch roosting sites can be completely covered with butterflies jostling for space and the sun's warmth.

I DON'T BELIEVE IT!
In 2009 monarch caterpillars were taken to the International Space Station. They became pupae and then adults onboard, fluttering in the weightless environment.

270 In spring the adults fly north and northeast. After a time they pause to breed, laying eggs that hatch after 3 to 8 days. The caterpillars eat milkweeds and similar plants that contain distasteful substances, which make them taste awful – as shown by their warning colours of yellow, white and black.

▶ Monarch caterpillars grow fast, reaching almost 5 centimetres in length.

BUTTERFLIES & MOTHS

▶ The pupa hangs from a twig by a silk thread.

① Fat, mature monarch caterpillars pupate. During this time of metamorphosis their bodies develop into adults.

② Body parts, such as the wings and abdomen, are visible on the pupa.

③ An adult monarch emerges. Its body is still soft and will have to harden before the butterfly can take flight and continue its migration.

271 After moulting five times over 9 to 16 days, the caterpillars become green pupae. After another 9 to 15 days the adults emerge, continue their northward migration, then stop and breed to produce another generation. This can happen three or four times in the same migration, as adult monarchs only live for 2 to 6 weeks. Some monarchs reach as far north as Canada, 4000 kilometres from the winter roosts.

272 Towards the end of summer, the final generation of adults make one non-stop flight back to the roost sites. In doing this, they avoid the harsh northern winter. This is the longest journey of any insect, and even of most creatures. After a winter rest, the whole cycle begins again.

◀ This map shows the main migration routes of monarchs across North America.

273 Such long-distance migrations may have begun long ago when the butterflies' roost sites were close to their feeding areas. Over time, climate and other changes separated these areas, and the butterflies gradually developed greater power and strength in flight.

We are the champions

274 Butterflies and moths are some of the largest insects. The species with the greatest wingspan is the white witch moth of Central and South America, at 30 centimetres or more. The Hercules moth of Southeast Asia and Australia, and the Atlas moth also of Southeast Asia, have wingspans of about 28 centimetres. However, they have the largest wing area, up to 400 square centimetres.

Greatest wingspan

ACTUAL SIZE

▶ The white witch moth is also called the giant ghost moth.

275 The giant carpenter moth of Australia is the heaviest adult butterfly or moth. It weighs up to 20 grams. But it is only half as heavy as the Atlas moth caterpillar, which can weigh over 50 grams.

Heaviest

▲ Atlas moth caterpillars weigh twice as much as the adult moths.

Smallest

ACTUAL SIZE

276 Tiniest butterflies include the Western pygmy blue of North America, with a wingspan of 1.5 centimetres. Far smaller are pygmy leaf-miner moths of the Nepticulidae family. Living in many regions but especially Australia and southern Asia, the feather-like wings of some species measure just 3 millimetres across.

▶ The white area of this bramble leaf shows where a golden pygmy moth caterpillar has eaten through it. The caterpillar grew as it ate.

BUTTERFLIES & MOTHS

277 The hungriest caterpillars are those of the polyphemus moth of North America. In less than two months they eat more than 60,000 times their own weight in leafy food – that's about the same as a person eating five million lettuces.

HANGING MOBILE

You will need:
thin card   colouring pencils
scissors   chopsticks, dowels or
similar   thin string

Find some pictures of the record-holding butterflies and moths featured on these pages. Draw them life-size on card, cut them out and colour them in. Attach them to the chopsticks or dowels with string to make a hanging mobile – which will need plenty of room!

278 The Arctic woolly bear moth has the longest life cycle – it takes seven years to develop from egg to adult. Almost all of this is spent in the hairy 'woolly bear' caterpillar stage. Due to chemicals produced in its body, the caterpillar can stand being frozen solid for up to 11 months each year, thawing out to feed for a few weeks, then freezing again. This happens around seven times before the caterpillar is ready to pupate.

Longest life cycle

▼ The Arctic caterpillar has natural 'anti-freeze' substances in its blood. When temperatures start to drop, it spins a protective cocoon in which it stays until it thaws out.

Evolution long ago

279 Like all animals, butterflies and moths have developed over time. We know this from their fossils – remains preserved in rock. The first moth fossils date back to the time of the early dinosaurs – the Jurassic Period, almost 200 million years ago. One of the earliest was *Archaeolepis*, a moth with a wingspan of about one centimetre. Its wing scales and other features were similar to the moth and butterfly cousins, caddisflies.

280 One of the earliest butterflies was the beautifully patterned *Prodryas*. It was fossilized about 40 million years ago during the Paleogene Period. With wings 1–2 centimetres long, it was a relative of today's mapwing and admiral butterflies, in the nymphalid family.

▼ *Prodryas*, with a wingspan of 2.5 centimetres, resembled today's mapwings, like the little map shown here.

281 Moth fossils become more varied from the start of the Cretaceous Period, around 145 million years ago. This was also when the first flowers evolved. As new kinds of flowers developed, new species of lepidopterans evolved to feed on them, such as tiger moths.

◀ Magnolias were among the first flowers to appear.

BUTTERFLIES & MOTHS

I DON'T BELIEVE IT!
Tiny preserved moth wing scales have been found in the stomachs of fossilized lizards from over 100 million years ago!

◀ Baltic amber from 40 million years ago has preserved all parts of this moth – even the contents of its gut.

282 Butterflies and moths have been perfectly preserved by being trapped in amber. This is the yellow or gold-coloured fluid known as resin that oozes from certain trees and then hardens. Amber from the Baltic region in Europe shows many kinds of butterflies and moths from 50–40 million years ago.

Habitats galore

283 Butterflies and moths, like most kinds of living things, thrive best in warm, damp climates. The tropical rainforest habitats around the middle of the Earth are hot or warm all year, with plenty of moisture that encourages plants and flowers. There are more kinds of butterflies and moths here than in all other habitats combined.

▼ Several kinds of blue morpho butterflies live in Central and South America.

284 To attract mates, tropical butterflies and moths often have brilliant patterns. These help them stand out even among the bright flowers and other colourful creatures. One of the shiniest is the blue morpho butterfly, with bright blue wings that catch the light. The wings of the harmonia mantle butterfly contain almost every colour of the rainbow.

Owl butterfly
Habitat: Dense lowland rainforest
Range: Southern North America to northern South America

Dirce beauty butterfly
Habitat: Open rainforest, shrubland
Range: Central and northern South America

Postman butterfly
Habitat: Open forest, scattered woodland
Range: Central America to southern Brazil

QUIZ
1. In what type of climates do butterflies and moths thrive?
2. How do species in tropical rainforests attract mates?
3. Why are tropical grassland species powerful fliers?

Answers:
1. Warm and damp 2. They have brilliant patterns 3. They search for flowers among the grasses

▲ The tropics extend either side of the Equator around the middle of the Earth, and harbour the world's richest wildlife.

BUTTERFLIES & MOTHS

▲ Tropical wetlands provide many places for 'puddling' — including the head of this caiman, a type of crocodile.

285 Tropical wetlands such as mangrove swamps are home to thousands of species. Many kinds, such as the Sunderbans crow butterfly, breed when water levels are low, and plants grow well. When the rainy season brings floods, they migrate to drier areas.

Rajah Brooke's birdwing butterfly
Habitat: Thick rainforest
Range: Southeast Asia

Comet moth
Habitat: Dense to open rainforest
Range: Madagascar

286 Species that live in tropical grasslands are generally powerful fliers as they have to search for flowers among the grasses. With a wingspan of 2 centimetres, the male African wild silkmoth is half the size of the female and flies more swiftly. People collect the threads from its cocoons and make them into silken fabrics.

▼ Just one silkmoth cocoon can produce a thread of raw silk up to one kilometre long.

287 Another kind of moth that spins a silken cocoon is the mulberry silk moth. Its caterpillars, or 'silkworms', eat mulberry tree leaves. For thousands of years its cocoons have been used to make the finest silk fabrics — a business worth £300 million each year. However due to centuries of special breeding, these moths must spend their whole life cycle in captivity. In their natural habitat they would perish from heat, cold, predators and disease.

From mountains to cities

288 Temperate woodland is a rich habitat for butterflies and moths. These areas have a warm spring and summer, and cool autumn and winter. Various species' life cycles are timed to allow them to feed on leaves as caterpillars, and then on flowers as adults. Across Europe and Asia, the brimstone is one of the first butterflies on the wing each year. It spends the winter as an adult hibernating in vegetation, and may wake up on a warmer day even with snow still on the ground.

▼ The meadow brown butterfly lives among grasslands, fields, orchards, parks and gardens.

▶ There are temperate areas throughout the world, providing rich habitats for butterflies and moths.

Woodland skipper
Habitat: Woods, shrubland, grassland
Range: West to central North America

289 Meadows and pastures have many adult butterflies and moths in early summer when most flowers are in bloom. However one of the most common, the meadow brown, can be active at any time from early spring to later autumn. It has a huge range across Europe, North Africa and Asia, and its caterpillars eat more than 20 different kinds of grasses.

BUTTERFLIES & MOTHS

◀ Buckthorn shrubs are the brimstone caterpillar's only food plant. The adult has a more varied diet.

290 Heaths, moors and mountains are also home to a variety of butterfly and moth species. In North America the Rocky Mountain dotted blue butterfly depends mainly on buckwheat plants. The caterpillars eat the leaves, then the adults drink nectar from the flowers. High in the European Alps, the mountain apollo butterfly flies powerfully for kilometres, even in strong winds, to find flowers with nectar.

Orange-tip butterfly
Habitat: Fields and other open areas
Range: Temperate Europe and Asia

White plume moth
Habitat: Mixed, from woods to gardens
Range: Europe

Six-spot burnet moth
Habitat: Meadows, cliffs, dunes, hedges, wood edges
Range: Europe, East Asia

Plain tiger butterfly
Habitat: Open country from hills to deserts
Range: Southern Europe to Southeast Asia

▼ The mountain apollo butterfly ranges across Europe's uplands and mountains, from Spain to Central Asia.

I DON'T BELIEVE IT!

Caterpillars of the Isabella tiger moth have been found in plant tubs covered in snow, on a skyscraper 50 floors high in New York City, USA.

291 Butterflies and moths are often found in urban habitats in towns and cities, especially in gardens where people plant nectar-rich flowers. The buddleia, which grows on wasteland in cities, is also called the 'butterfly bush' because it attracts so many species (see page 95). In South Africa the caterpillars of the garden acraea butterfly eat wild peach tree leaves and the adults visit passion flowers – both popular urban plants.

Dangers past and present

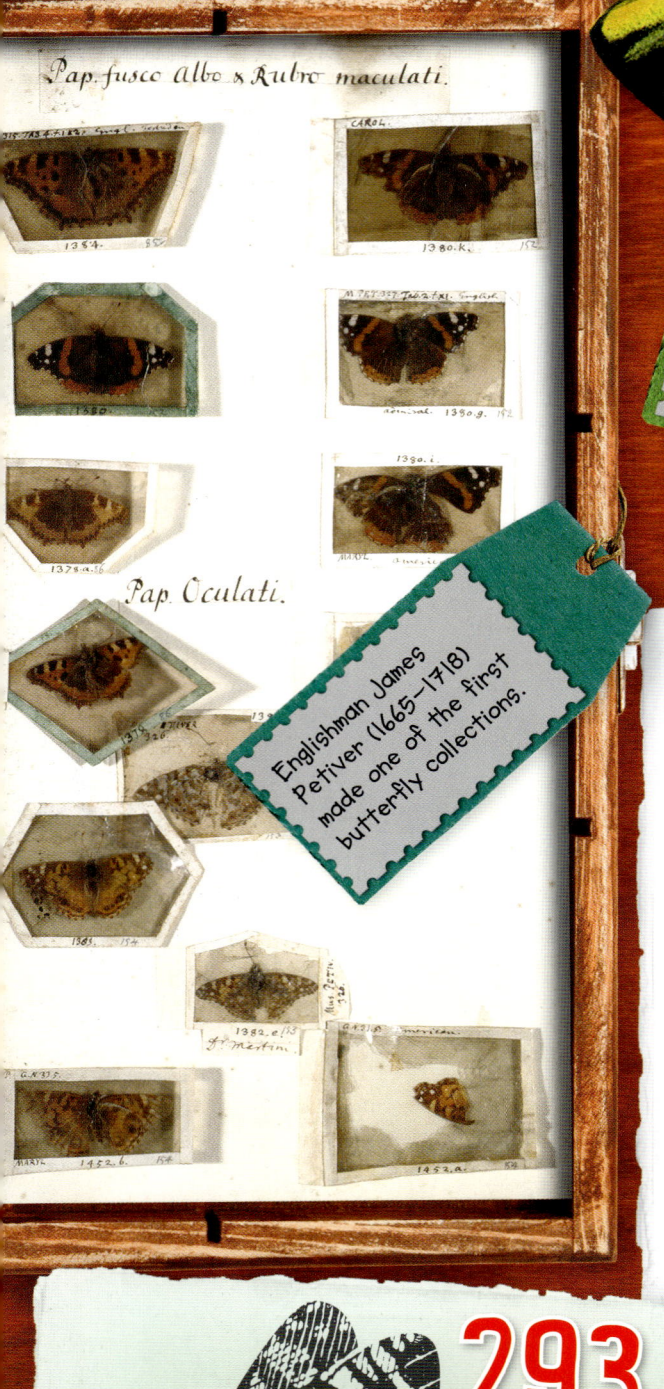

Queen Alexandra's birdwing, the world's largest butterfly, is endangered due to collecting.

Englishman James Petiver (1665–1718) made one of the first butterfly collections.

292 The scientific study of butterflies and moths began in 18th-century Europe. Its experts are known as lepidopterists. In the 19th century explorers travelled the world to catch specimens for collections and museums, making some species rare. It still occurs today, despite laws put in place to protect wildlife.

293 Habitat loss is a giant problem for many butterfly and moth species. Areas such as forests and wetlands are converted to houses, farms and factories. One of the first recorded extinctions caused by habitat loss was that of Sloane's urania moth of Jamaica. Already rare from collecting, it became extinct by 1910 as the island's lowland forests were cleared for timber and farmland.

The day-flying Sloane's urania moth was black with red, blue and green markings.

BUTTERFLIES & MOTHS

294 Also harmful are pesticide and herbicide chemicals, used to rid our food crops of pests and weeds. Caterpillars and adults are especially vulnerable when herbicides kill their food plants. Monarch butterflies have suffered due to loss of the milkweed plants they feed on. Non-chemical or biological control is a less damaging alternative. For example, parasites may be used to infest only the crop's pest species, leaving other plants and animals unharmed.

I DON'T BELIEVE IT!
The Palos Verde blue may be the rarest butterfly. It is only found in one small area of California, USA. Its habitat is now protected, but its numbers in the wild are just a few hundred.

295 Climate change is a threat to much wildlife, including butterflies and moths. For example, plants flowering earlier due to higher temperatures may mean the blooms are not around when adult butterflies or moths need to feed on them. This leads to 'uncoupling' of food chains, which can upset the entire balance of nature.

Edith's checkerspot butterfly of western North America is becoming rarer due to climate change.

Invasive plants such as crown vetch can crowd out local butterfly or moth food plants.

296 Other threats include non-native or alien species being introduced. The introduced species may be plants that smother a lepidopteran's local food plant, or a new predator. There may be introduced parasites such as tiny wasps or flies whose grubs (larvae) eat any life stage, or diseases caused by bacteria, viruses and moulds.

123

Hopes for the future

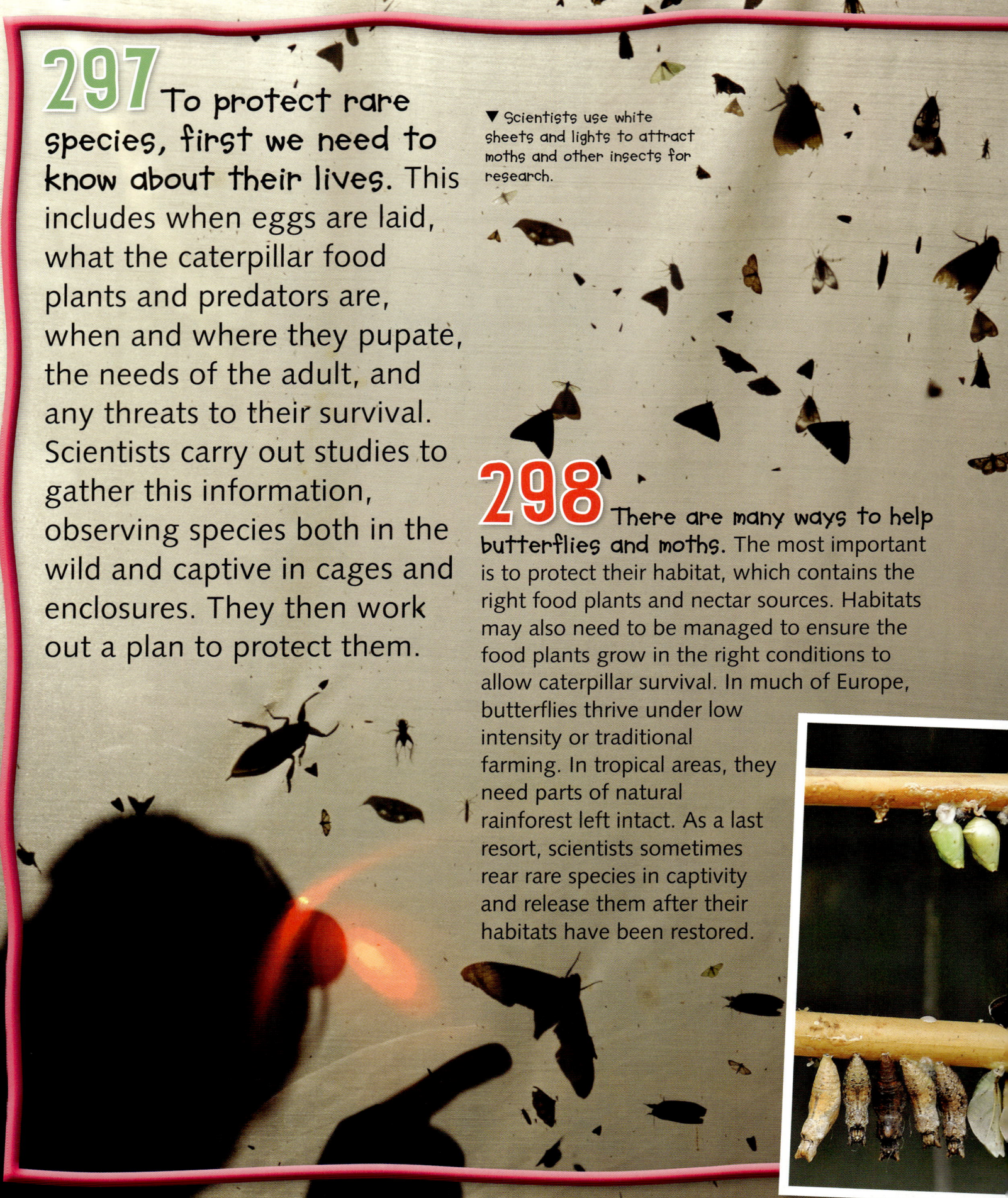

297 To protect rare species, first we need to know about their lives. This includes when eggs are laid, what the caterpillar food plants and predators are, when and where they pupate, the needs of the adult, and any threats to their survival. Scientists carry out studies to gather this information, observing species both in the wild and captive in cages and enclosures. They then work out a plan to protect them.

▼ Scientists use white sheets and lights to attract moths and other insects for research.

298 There are many ways to help butterflies and moths. The most important is to protect their habitat, which contains the right food plants and nectar sources. Habitats may also need to be managed to ensure the food plants grow in the right conditions to allow caterpillar survival. In much of Europe, butterflies thrive under low intensity or traditional farming. In tropical areas, they need parts of natural rainforest left intact. As a last resort, scientists sometimes rear rare species in captivity and release them after their habitats have been restored.

▶ Keen children learn how to use a butterfly net safely.

299 **Education is also vital.** People can be informed about the fascinating lives of butterflies and moths, and their importance to pollination and food chains. Butterfly houses, nature reserves and watching events raise awareness and encourage people to get involved.

300 **As individuals, we can all help butterflies and moths.** For example, it is easy to grow food plants for caterpillars and adults – anywhere from a windowbox to a large garden. Old leaves, log piles, weed patches and similar places are ideal for them to shelter during winter. Schools and clubs can also create butterfly gardens and similar projects. It all helps to conserve these beautiful, fascinating and vital creatures for the future.

MAKE A GARDEN

Find out about making a butterfly and moth garden. Packets of specially chosen 'butterfly mix' seeds can be sown in flowerpots, troughs, windowboxes or a corner of the garden, to provide food plants. Your local wildlife trust probably has a lepidopterist who can give advice.

◀ Captive breeding provides individuals to release into the wild.

Index

Entries in **bold** refer to main subject entries. Entries in *italics* refer to illustrations

A
abdomen 44, *44*, 45, 86, *86*, **91**, *91*
admiral butterflies **104**
adonis blue butterfly 96, *96*
adult butterfly (imago) **98**, 99, *99*
anatomy 44, *44*, **90–91**
ant beetle 32, *32*
ant-mimic spider 67
antennae (feelers), butterflies & moths 86, *86*, **89**, *89*, 90, *90*, **92**, *92*, **93**, 96
antlion 22
ants 9, *9*, 20, 27, *27*, **28–29**, 32
aphids 13, 24, 29
Apollo butterflies 12, *12*, 89, *89*, **105**, 121, *121*
arachnids 6, 38, 40, 80, **48–49**
arachnologists (spider scientists) 83
arachnophobia 80
Atlas moth 96, 103, 109, *109*, 110, 114, *114*
Australian redback spider 74, 75
Bagheera kiplingi spider 65

B
ballooning, spiders 52
beach wolf spider 58
bee fly 33
bees 9, 26, *26*, 28, 29, 33, *33*, 40, *40*
beetles 6, 8, 10, 13, 15, 17, 20, *21*, 24, 25, 27, 34, *38*, 40
bird dung spider 47
bird-dropping caterpillar 31, *31*
birdwing butterflies 86, **90–91**, **105**
bites 9, 12, **26–27**, 39
black widow spiders 74, *74*
blue butterflies 86, 97, **104**, 114, 123
blue morpho butterfly **118**, *118*
bogong moths 35, 111, *111*
bombardier beetle 27
Brazilian wandering spider 69
breeding **54–55**, **96–97**
brimstone butterflies 97, 120, *121*
bristletails 13
bumblebees 29
burnished brass moth 102, *102*
butterfly hawk moth 88

C
camouflage 23, 30, **106–107**, *107*
caterpillars (larvae) 8, 10, *10*, 21, 25, 31, **89**, **98**, *98*, 99, *99*, **100–101**, *100*, *101*, 114, *114*, 115, *115*, 119

cave spider 50, *58*
cecropia moth *110–111*
centipedes 39, *39*
cephalothorax 80, *80*
Charlotte's Web 81, *81*
chelicerae 80, *81*
chrysalis *see* pupa
cicadas 21, *21*, 37, *37*
claws 53
click beetle 15, *15*, 20, *21*
climate change **123**
cobweb spiders 74
cockchafers (chafers) 6, *6–7*, 21
cockroaches 16, *16*
cocoons 56, *56*, **89**, *89*, **99**, 115, 119, *119*
collecting, butterflies **122**, *122*
colonies **28–29**
colours 69, **87**, 108, *108*, 109, 112
comb-footed spiders 74
common mime butterfly 107, *107*
cooking, spiders 80, *80*
copper butterflies 86, **104**
courtship 10, 13, **97**, *97*
courtship dances, spiders 54–55
crab spiders 47, *47*, 50, 55, 65, 69, *69*
crane fly 21, *21*
crickets 11, *11*, **36–37**, *36–37*
cucumber spider 71
cutworm moths 110

D
daddy longlegs 21, *21*
daddy longlegs spiders 63, *63*
damselflies 19
defence, butterflies **101**, *101*
devil's coach-horse 17, *17*
diseases 41
draglines 66, 76
dragonflies 13, *13*, 19
dung beetles 25

E
earwig 8, *8*, 20
eating, spiders **64–65**
Edith's checkerspot butterfly 123
eggs 9, **10**, *10*, 25, 29, 41, 56, **98**, *98*
emperor butterflies 86, **104**, *104*
emperor moths 87, *88*, 103
European black widow spider 74
European tarantula 80
evolution, butterflies & moths **116–117**
exoskeleton 8, **90**, 98
extinction 83, **122**
eyes 8, 13, 32, 36, 44, 45, 50, *50*, 77, 86, *86*, 90, *90*, *92*, 92

eyesight, spiders 50, 51, 76, 79
eyespots 88, **108**, *108*

F
false scorpions 48
fangs 44, 45, 50, 64, 72, 79
feeding 57, 64–65, **94–95**
feet (tarsi) 53, *53*
firefly 13, *13*
fleas 15
flies 8, 9, 10, 12, *38*, 40
food plants 98, 123
fossils, butterflies & moths **116**, *116*, **117**
frenulum 89
fritillary butterflies 84, 86, **104**
froghopper *14–15*, 15
funnel web spiders 66, 67, **72–73**

G
garden spiders 45, **54–55**, **70–71**
geometer moths 87, 91, 93, **102**, *102*
giant carpenter moth 114
giant huntsman spider 46
gills 19
'glue' 61
gold leaf crab spider 65
golden orb-web spiders 71
golden wheel spider 66
Goliath bird-eating spiders 46, *46*, 78
grasshoppers 14, *14*
great diving beetle 19, *19–20*
great silver water beetle 19
green lynx spider 64
green tiger beetle 17
green tree ants 61
grubs 10, 20, *21*, 24, 25

H
habitats **58–59**, 82, 84, **118–121**, 124
hairs 50, 53, *53*, 68, 79, *79*
hairstreak butterflies 86, **104**
harvestmen 48, 49, *49*
hawk moth 87, **103**, *103*
hawk wasp 79
hedylid butterflies **105**, *105*
herbicides **123**
Hercules moth 114
hesperiid butterflies 86, **104**, *104*
hibernation **34**, 58, 120
honeybees 29, 40, *40*
hornet 26, *26*, 33, *33*
hornet moth 33, *33*
horsefly 8
house spiders 52, 83
housefly 8

hoverfly 32
hunting spiders **68–69**, 76

IJK
instar 98, *98*, 99
iridescence **87**
irruptions **111**
jumping spiders 50, 54, **76–77**, *76–77*
katipo 74
king baboon spider 78, *78*

L
labyrinth spider 73, *73*
lacebug 25
lacewing 22, *22*
ladybird spider 82, *82*
ladybirds 8, *8*, 34, *34–35*
larvae 10, 11, *17*, 20, 21, *21*, 22, 24, *24*, 25, 28, 29, *29*
leaf-miner moth 110
leafcutter ants 28
leatherjacket 21, *21*
legs 44, 51, 67, 72, 86, *86*, 90, **91**, 100, *100*
Lepidoptera **86–87**, *86–87*
life cycle, butterflies & moths **98–99**, *98–99*, 115
locusts 35, *35*
looper caterpillar 87, *100*, **102**, *102*
loss of **122**
lycaenid butterflies 86, **104**, *104*
lynx spider 59, *64*

M
maggots 10
malaria 41
mayflies 19
meadow brown butterfly **120**, *120*
mealybugs 24
metamorphosis 11, **98–99**, *98–99*
Mexican red-knee tarantula 50, *79*
midges 12
midget spider 47, *71*
migration **35**, **111**, *111*, 112–113, *113*
millipedes 6, 39, *39*
mimicry **32–33**, **108–109**, *108, 109*
mites 38, *38*, 40, 48, *48*
mole cricket 37, *37*
monarch butterflies 33, *33*, 34, 86, **104**, 111, **112–113**, *112, 113*, 123
money spiders 63
moon moths 87, *87*
mosquitoes 12, 41, *41*
moth families **102–103**
moth larvae 61
moulting 11, *11*, 57, *57*, **98**, 99

mouse spiders 68
mouthparts 22, 90, 94, 100, *100*
movement, spiders **52–53**

N
net-casting spiders *see* ogre-faced spider
no-eyed big-eyed wolf spiders 83
noctuid (owlet) moths 87, 93, **102**
nocturnal spiders 51
nursery-web spiders 56, *56*
nymphalid butterflies 86, **104**, *104*, 116
nymphs 11, 17, *17*, 19, *19*

O
ogre-faced spider 50, *51*
orb-web spiders **70–71**, *70–71*
orbweaver spiders 62, 65
ornate jumping spiders 55

P
paper kite butterfly 97, *97*
papilionid butterflies 86, **105**, *105*
peacock butterflies 93, 98
peacock parachute spider 82, *82*
peacock spiders 47, *47*
pedipalps 44, 45
peppered moth 106, *106*
pesticides **123**
pests 95
pets 80
pheromones **89**, 92, **96**
pierid butterflies 86, **105**
playing dead 67, *67*
poison *see* venom
pollination **40**
polyphemus moth **115**
pondskaters 18, *18*
praying mantis 10, 23, *23*
predators, avoiding **66–67**
proboscis **90**, *90*, **94**, *94*, 95
puddling 95, *95*
pupa (chrysalis) **89**, *89*, **98**, **99**, *99*, **107**, *107*, 113, *113*
pupae **11**, *11*, 21, 29
purple emperor butterfly 97, *97*
puss moth caterpillar 101, *101*
pygmy leaf-miner moth 114, *114*

Q R
Queen Alexandra's birdwing butterfly *122*
raft spiders 53, *53*
red admiral butterfly 98
red velvet mites 48

regal moth 103, *103*
riodinid butterflies 86, **105**, *105*

S
saturnid moths **103**, *103*
scaffold web spiders 54
scale insects *24*
scales **87**, *87*, 91, *91*, 117
scopulae 53
scorpion venom 49
scorpionfly 9
scorpions 38, 40, 48, *48*
senses **50–51**, **92–93**
sheet webs 63, *63*
shield bug 24, 30, *30*
silk 41, *41*, 81, 60, **60–61**, *62*
silk glands 62
silk moths 87, **119**, *119*
silverfish 13, *13*
skipjack 15
skipper butterflies 86, **104**, 110, *120*
slit organs 50
Sloane's urania moth 122, *122*
social spiders 59
solifuge 45
songs 36
sphinx moths 87, *94*, **103**
Spider-Man 81, *81*
spiderlings **56–57**, *56–57*
spigots 62, *62*
spinnerets 44, 45, *45*, 62
spitting spiders 41, *41*, 50, 68, *68*
springtail 14
stick insects 31, *31*
stings 9, **26–27**, 32, *32*
stoneflies 17, *17*, 19
sun-spiders 49, *49*
swallowtail butterflies 86, 98–99, **105**, *105*, 107, *107*, 109
Sydney funnel web spider *72*

T
tarantella dance 80
tarantulas 26, *26*, 50, 78, **78–79**, *79*, 80, **80**, 82
taste, spiders 50, 51
termites 20, 28, 29
thornbugs 30, *30*
ticks 38, *38*, 40, 48, *48*
tiger butterflies *108*, 121
tiger moths 87, 89, 93, *101*, 116, 121
tortoiseshell butterflies 95, 98
trapdoor spiders 69, *69*
trapping spiders 70–71
traps 51, 62, 63

tube-web spiders 73, *73*
tympanal organs **93**

U V
ultraviolet light 92, *93*
underwing moths 87, 111
venom (poison) 49, *64*, 68, *72*, 74, 81
venom (poison) gland 69, *80*
vibration 50
viceroy butterfly 11, 33, *33*

W
wandering spiders **68–69**
woolly bear caterpillars **101**, *101*, **115**, *115*
warning colours 88, 101, **108**, 109, 112

wasps 9, *22*, 26, 28, 29, *29*, 32, 79, *79*
water spiders 58, 59, *59*
weaver ants 61, *61*
web-building 70
webs 51, *56*, 60–61, 62, 63, **70–71**
white butterflies 86, 110
white witch moth 114, *114*
wings 6, 8, *8*, 11, **12**, 14, *15*, 38, 86, *86*, 87, *87*, 88, 89, *90*, **91**, *91*, **110–111**, *110*, *111*
wireworm 20, *21*

wolf spiders *42–43*, 52, 55, 57, *57*, **75**, *75*
wood ants 29
woodlice 39, *39*
woodworms *24*

ACKNOWLEDGEMENTS

The publishers would like to thank the following sources for the use of their photographs:

Key: t = top, b = bottom, l = left, r = right, c = centre, bg = background

Alamy 56(b) Susan & Allan Parker; 59 Corbis Premium RF; 73(t) Brian Hewitt; 117 The Natural History Museum; 122(l) The Natural History Museum; 123(cl) Robert Rosenblum; 125(tr) ZUMA Press, Inc
Ardea 56 Brian Bevan; 73(b) Steve Hopkin
Corbis 64 Robert Marien; 102(b) Frans Hodzelmans/NIS/Minden Pictures; 103(c) Visuals Unlimited; 106(bl) Stephen Dalton/Minden Pictures; 112(l) Frans Lanting; 119(tl) Frank Krahmer/Masterfile
Dreamstime 35(bc) Paop; 56(t) Cathykeifer; 60 Cathykeifer; 80(t) Thierry; 98(c) Gordzam; 100(bl) Sakda Nokkaew; 108(bl) Hakoar
FLPA 24(t) Bob Gibbons; 27(bc) Christian Ziegler/Minden Pictures; 32(bc) Alfred Schauhuber/Imagebroker; 37(b) Albert Visage; 49 Piotr Naskrecki/Minden Pictures; 50 Mark Moffett/Minden Pictures; 51 Michael & Patricia Fogden/Minden Pictures; 54 Mark Moffett/Minden Pictures; 58(b) Larry West; 61 Thomas Marent/Minden Pictures; 62(r) Richard Becker; 63(t) Heidi & Hans-Juergen Koch/Minden Pictures; 79(t) and (b) Mark Moffett/Minden Pictures; 87(c) Thomas Marent/Minden Pictures; 88(tl) Konrad Wothe/Minden Pictures; 89(tl) Michael Durham/Minden Pictures; 96(c) Arik Siegel/Nature in Stock; 97(b) Michael & Patricia Fogden/Minden Pictures; 99(b) Silvia Reiche/Minden Pictures; 105(b) Imagebroker, Adam Seward/Imagebroker; 113(bg) Ingo Arndt/Minden Pictures; 120(bl) Matt Cole 118(tr) Piotr Naskrecki/Minden Pictures; 86–87(t, tr) deardone; 112(tr, bg)
Fotolia 64 Liv Friis-larsen; 86–87(t, tr) Morley Read; Alexey Khromushin
iStockphoto.com 5(b) Atelopus; 42–43 Morley Read; 77 ElementalImaging; 88(tr) KirsanovV; 107(br) Diana Meister; 114(cl) CatherineSim; 121(tl) Tree4Two
Moviestore Collection 81(t) Paramount Pictures, Walden Media, K Entertainment Company, Nickelodeon Movies, KMP Film Invest, Sandman Studios
National Geographic Creative 104(b) Darlyne A. Murawski; 119(bl) Cary Wolinsky
Nature Picture Library 10(tr) Meul/ARCO; 13(bl) Nature Production; 14(c) Stephen Dalton; 15(tl) Stephen Dalton; 17(c) Visuals Unlimited; 30(r) John Cancalosi; 53(b) Stephen Dalton; 54–55 Simon Colmer; 58(t) Stephen Dalton; 62(l) Ingo Arndt; 63(b) Nick Upton; 66 Solvin Zankl; 71 Stephen Dalton; 76–77 Kim Taylor; 83 Stephen Dalton; 85 Paul Harcourt Davies; 95(tr) ARCO; 114(b) Paul Hobson; 121(cr) Paul Harcourt Davies; 124 Shibai Xiao; 125(b) Adrian Davies
NHPA 67 Stephen Dalton; 75 A.N.T. Photo Library; 78 Jany Sauvanet
Photoshot 80(b) Imagebroker/Everett; 111(tr) Finlayson/Newspix
Rex Features 81(b) Columbia/Everett
Science Photo Library 37(b) Thomas & Pat Leeson; 91(br) Susumu Nishinaga; 92–93(b) Cordelia Molloy
Shutterstock.com back cover Andrey Pavlov (ants), NH (rhinoceros beetle), Rob Hainer (dragonfly), sydeen (spider), Sean van Tonder (grasshopper), aaltair (butterfly), irin-k (ladybird), 1 CHAINFOTO24 (beetle), Cathy Keifer (moth), Andrey Snegirev (bee), Amy Prentice (grasshopper), wanida tubtawee (butterfly); 2–3 Cathy Keifer; 4–5 Tomatito; 5(t) vblinov, 5(r) Cathy Keifer; 9(r) Tan Hung Meng; 11(bc) Geanina Bechea; 12(bl) jps, (c) Marco Uliana; 15(br) Mark Carrel; 16(c) Smit; 18(tr) Sue Robinson; 19(tr) Dirk Ercken; 21(br) Steve Byland; 22(tr) jcwait; 24(bl) dabjola, (cl) Rasmus Holmboe Dahl; 25(tr) Nick Stubbs, (bc) Henrik Larsson; 29(tl) Csati; 31(cl) Matt Jeppson, (t) IrinaK; 36(c) Narisa Koryanyong; 32(bg) Triff; 33(cr) xpixel, (cl) Glenn Jenkinson; 36(c) Eric Isselee; 38(cl) r. classen; 45(l) and (r) BHJ; 46(c) LilKar; 47(bl) npouard Rozey; 48(br) Tobik; 52(t) ctpaul; 69 Lidara; 70–71 Dean Pennala; 84 aabeele; 85(tr) Andreas Weitzmann; 88(tc) Matthijs Wetterauw, (bl) Frank Hoekzema, (bc) AleksandarMilutinovic, (br) Kirsanov Valeriy Vladimirovich, (bc) bigfatcat, (cr) nuttakit; 98(b) Krzysztof Slusarczyk; 98–99(t) jps; 99(t) and (c) jps; 100(tr) Mathisa; 101(cr) Hugh Lansdown, (bl) neil hardwick; 102(tr) twospeeds; 103(bl) Rob Hainer; 104(tr) M. Shcherbyna; 105(tl) Matee Nuserm; 106(bl) tobkatrina; 107(tl) Tyler Fox; 108–109(t) Melinda Fawver; 109(tl) Kaulitzki, (br) Paul van den Berg; 110–111(m) Cathy Keifer; 112(br) Steve Brigman; 113(t) StevenRussellSmithPhotos, (cl) KPG_Payless; 114–115(c) guentermanaus; 116(cr) Matee Nuserm, (bl) S_Photo; 118(map, t) hagit berkovich, (map, c) Dennis van de Water, (map, b) Ammit Jack; 119 (map, l) Andreas Weitzmann, (map, r) Ivan Hor; 120(map) Randimal; 121(map, tl) A.S.Floro, (map, cl) aaltair, (map, cr) Bildagentur Zoonar GmbH, (map, b) Matee Nuserm; v122(bl) Morphart Creation; 123(t) grintan, (r) My Good Images, (bc) Evoken
SuperStock.com 98(t) imageBROKER/imageBROKER

All other photographs are from: digitalSTOCK, digitalvision, ImageState, iStockphoto.com, John Foxx, PhotoAlto, PhotoDisc, PhotoEssentials, PhotoPro, Shutterstock.com, Stockbyte, Wikipedia Commons

Every effort has been made to acknowledge the source and copyright holder of each picture. Miles Kelly Publishing apologizes for any unintentional errors or omissions.

Cover illustration Peter Bull Art Studio